There are so many rules and regulations surrounding the green jacket, one of the most exclusive items of clothing in the world, that few know about. *(Oliver Katcher)*

Jennifer Kupcho won the Augusta National Women's Amateur tournament in 2019. The tournament debuted in 2019. Augusta National first began admitting women as members in 2012. *(AP Images)*

The Spanish golfer known as El Niño finally got the monkey off his back in 2017 when he won his first Masters. *(AP Images)*

Rory McIlroy is still looking for his first Masters win. His best result was finishing fourth in 2015. *(AP Images)*

Arnold Palmer has the iconic green jacket draped over his shoulders by Jack Nicklaus after winning the 1964 Masters. *(AP Images)*

Mike Weir helps Phil Mickelson into his green jacket after his first Masters win in 2004. *(AP Images)*

The clubhouse at Augusta National, located near the first tee, dates back to the 1850s. *(Oliver Katcher)*

One of the first images the Masters brings to mind for many are gorgeous azaleas in full bloom. *(Oliver Katcher)*

The massive oak tree that sits between the iconic white clubhouse and the first tee is the oldest living member of Augusta National. *(Oliver Katcher)*

For many people, the Par-3 Contest held on the Wednesday before the Masters each year is more notable than the tournament itself. *(Oliver Katcher)*

The 1997 Masters was Tiger Woods' first as a professional. Needless to say, it would not be his last. *(AP Images)*

His victory in the 2015 Masters also happened to be Jordan Spieth's first major win. *(AP Images)*

Sergio Garcia congratulates Patrick Reed (left), 2018 Masters champion. It was Reed's first major win. *(AP Images)*

Tiger Woods' triumphant victory in the 2019 Masters made for one of the best comeback stories in sports history. *(AP Images)*

The year before, Palmer's final appearance at Augusta in 2016, and his final visit to the first tee for the Thursday morning tradition, Palmer's health had been in decline and there were questions about whether he'd be able to hit a shot alongside Nicklaus and Player.

"I think that everybody was happy to see Arnold out on the tee," Nicklaus said at the time. "I think Arnold was happy to be on the tee. I think he would have preferred to hit a golf ball. I talked to him at the Masters Champions Dinner [two nights earlier] and I said, 'Arnold, when you're out there, what if we just take you up and had you hit, I don't care if you putt it off the tee, I think everybody would love to have you do anything.'

"He said, 'Let me think about it.' I said, 'Okay.' So [that Thursday] morning, I talked to him and I said, 'What do you want to do?' He said, 'I'm good.' I said, 'Fine, let's leave it alone.' So I think probably the right thing. Arnold's balance is not good and that's what they were worried about. But I think he was delighted to be out there. I think we were delighted to have him there. I think both Gary and I felt it was more about Arnold [that] morning than anything else and I think that was just fine."

Curtis Strange, the two-time U.S. Open winner who went to Wake Forest, where Palmer went to school, said the Masters "will never be the same" without The King.

"The tournament will go on and players will come and go, but there will be a void there," Strange said. "I grew up with Arnold Palmer in my household as everybody did. And then the first time I played the Masters was in '75. I went down there and saw really what Arnie's Army and Arnold Palmer and the people were all about. It was the first time I had ever seen him in his world. And it was spectacular.

"There was a connection there between Arnold and the people and the people and Arnold that was unlike anything I had ever seen in my life before and since. The way he reacted to them and them to him was something special. And even [in 2016], when he wasn't doing well, and just for him to make the effort to go and be a part of it, something he loved so dearly, it showed me that it really was a connection there over the years and that they truly loved each other."

Andy North, like Strange a two-time U.S. Open champion, adored Palmer like everyone else. And, like everyone who attended the Masters, whether as a player, spectator, or member of the media, he could not wait to see Palmer hit one of those ceremonial first tee shots every year, because it made him feel like he was a part of something special, something historic.

"I remember as a kid, really the first time you ever saw golf on TV, or at least I did, was Arnold," North said. "That changed the way we looked at our sport. The last year he played there, I'm one of those guys that used to go out on Thursday morning and love watching the guys hit those first tee shots. That was always special. And there's going to be a big empty spot at the Masters because Arnold's not there."

Nantz recalled Palmer, in 2016 at his final Masters, agreeing to come to Butler Cabin to be interviewed after what would be his final appearance for that ceremonial first tee shot.

Nantz had asked Palmer about doing the interview weeks earlier and they agreed, because of Palmer's failing health, that they'd wait to decide until that Thursday morning to see if Palmer was up for the taping.

"I met him in the clubhouse after the shot and we're sitting around a table and he looked at me and said, 'What do you think?' I said, 'It's totally up to you,'" Nantz recalled. "And he looked at me and gave me that Arnie thumbs-up and said, 'Let's do it.' So we got the Butler Cabin ready to go and got Arnold to the cabin and we made it very clear if it was a struggle or the words wouldn't come out cleanly we'd stop and no one would ever see it.

"When the lights went on and the first question was about showing up here in 1955, it was like turning back the clock. You could see the look on his face. When the lights came on, Arnold was on."

Nantz, who has witnessed and called some of the most memorable moments that have ever occurred at Augusta National, said that moment was one he'll "never forget."

"He never returned," Nantz said. "That was his last visit to the Masters."

PART FIVE

FRIDAY

Chapter 14

ARNIE

F ew sporting events in the world produce moments like the Masters does at Augusta National every April. These moments have become a rite of springtime and they often spawn memories of a lifetime for those fortunate enough to witness them in person or even through a television screen.

On Friday afternoon, April 10, 2004, at about 2:15 PM, one of those unforgettable moments unfolded simultaneously on holes No. 6 and No. 16, where the two greens are half a sand wedge apart, separated by only spectators, pine needles, and a few tall pine trees.

The hill situated below the sixth tee and overlooking the 16th green, where fans sprawl out on the grass as if they were chilling out at Jones Beach on an 80-degree day watching the waves roll in off the Atlantic, is one of the finest places in sports to watch the action unfold.

While Jack Nicklaus was arriving at the 16th green, Arnold Palmer, playing in his 50th consecutive—and final—Masters, had just stuck his tee shot to within five feet of the flag on the sixth green to the delight of the throng of fans packed into the area.

Then, as Nicklaus was surveying his 30-foot birdie putt on the 16th green, Palmer and his larger-than-life image were silhouetted against the afternoon sun as he walked over the top of the hill and headed down toward the sixth green. Nicklaus, now watching Palmer, removed his cap and lifted it in the air in honor of The King and then gave him the thumbs up, a customary Palmer gesture.

Palmer, catching eyes with Nicklaus, returned the love, taking his cap off, giving the thumbs up and waving. The place was delirious.

Moments later, Nicklaus and Palmer were standing over their respective putts at the exact same moment, Nicklaus sinking his three-footer for par and Palmer barely missing his five-foot birdie attempt and tapping in for par.

With that being Palmer's final round of his final Masters, it was the last time a moment like that would ever play out, and it was one to be forever inscribed into the memory banks for all who were there to see it.

It was the best of all Masters moments on the Friday of the 68th edition of the storied event.

About three hours after that memorable moment, which would not be captured on television, because back then the front nine of the Masters was not televised, Palmer would amble his way up the steep, uphill 18th fairway to the green for the last time at a Masters at age 74.

Palmer, winner of four green jackets, all coming in a dizzying seven-year span, was playing in his 50th and final Masters, shooting a pair of 84s on his way to missing the cut.

"I'm not going to make a big, long speech today," Palmer said. "I'm through. I've had it. I'm done. Cooked. Washed up. Finished, whatever you want to say. It's time."

When asked what it felt like to walk up 18 for one final time at Augusta, Palmer said, "Use your imagination, and you will understand. I thought about how many times I walked up that 18th fairway. I can think of the four times I won the Masters. I can think of a couple of times that I didn't win that I felt like I should have won.

"I can think of the fans that have supported me. I listened to them, and of course most of them have something to say when I'm walking up that fairway. Emotion? A lot. Sometimes I just get tired and emotion overrules and runs away with me. I'm not upset about that. The fact is that one of the things I want to do was what I did today, and that was to finish 50 years at Augusta. All my family is here, and that has never happened before at any golf tournament. That's very special. It's something I wanted. I just wanted them to see what happens."

Palmer went on to say, "Augusta and this golf tournament has been about [as much] a part of my life as anything other than my family. I don't think I could ever separate myself from this club and this tournament. I may not be present, I may not be here, but I'll still be a part of what happens here, only because I want to be."

Palmer was a presence at the Masters for 62 years—50 as a player, 10 as an honorary starter, and two more years for the time in between when he wasn't sure he wanted to hit the ceremonial first tee shot as an honorary starter.

The 2017 Masters was the first since 1954 Palmer was not in attendance, and it was an emotional week because of it. The highlight of the week was a powerful ceremony at the first tee led by then-chairman Billy Payne, who had an empty chair set up in honor of The King with his green jacket draped over the back of it.

"It will never be the same," said Curtis Strange, who had a special bond with Palmer because of their Wake Forest connection. (Strange went to Wake Forest on an Arnold Palmer Scholarship established by The King at his alma mater.)

Palmer was the first player to win the Masters four times. Jack Nicklaus would eventually break his record with six and Tiger Woods overtook him in 2019 when he won his fifth. But Palmer could have had more.

In 1959, as the defending champion, he was tied for the lead after three rounds. But Palmer made a triple-bogey at the par-3 12th and finished third that year, two shots behind winner Art Wall Jr., who started the day six shots behind Palmer.

In 1961, Palmer was vying to become the tournament's first repeat winner, needing only a par at the 72nd to give him a one-shot victory over Gary Player. But Palmer hit his approach shot from the fairway into a greenside bunker and then bladed his next shot across the green and took a double bogey to lose by one shot to Player.

It was Palmer's play around holes No. 11, 12, and 13 on the far corner of Augusta National in 1958 en route to his first Masters win that inspired *Sports Illustrated* writer Herbert Warren Wind to use the expression "Amen Corner" to describe those three iconic holes.

"Arnie's Army," the nickname used to describe the horde of spectators following Palmer as if he were a pied piper, was born in Augusta because of the soldiers at nearby Fort Gordon who manned the leaderboards at the Masters and openly rooted for Palmer.

The late Frank Chirkinian, the pioneering TV producer who ran the Masters telecasts on CBS for 40 years, once described how Palmer had become a magnet to the camera during his back-nine charge in 1960, saying, "I thought, 'Holy mackerel, who is this guy?' He absolutely fired up the screen. It was quite obvious this was the star. It was electrifying."

Chapter 15

DALY

It is late afternoon on the eve of the Masters, a little after 6:00 PM on Wednesday. The annual Par-3 Contest is long finished. The players' practice rounds have been completed.

And yet, there is a line of fans snaking through a parking lot waiting to purchase merchandise. The people are not lined up to buy Masters souvenirs, though. They are not even on Augusta National property.

They are in a Hooters parking lot, located about three or four John Daly tee shots down Washington Road from Magnolia Lane, patiently waiting to meet Daly, shake his hand, express their love for him, and score items from the John Daly brand.

There are boxes of "Grip it and Rip it" T-shirts, logoed ball markers, head covers, license plates, hats, CDs, pin flags, towels, beverage coozies, belts, and Loudmouth apparel, including shorts and skorts. There, too, are cans of Daly's branded "Grip it and Sip it" beverages made with iced tea and vodka or sweet tea, lemonade, and vodka.

Most importantly, the people are there to meet Daly, have him sign autographs, express their adulation for him, and take selfies with them.

Daly has been posted up with his RV and a bunch of tables with his merchandise outside the gates of Augusta National during Masters week since 1997, hawking souvenirs.

With a cigarette hanging limply from his lips, he engages with all who stop by. And, if you buy it, he'll sign it. He'll actually sign anything you ask him to—whether you've made a purchase or not.

"I've probably signed about 20 sets of boobs this week and about 30 asses," Daly said as he signed for fans in line rapid-fire before the 2018 Masters. "And they are fine asses, too. I'll sign any ass, it doesn't matter. Like Jesus, I love 'em all."

It is an unmistakable sideshow bordering on a carnival act—as it always has been since Daly first started doing this.

"I just figured it's a good way to sell the brand," Daly said while signing the package of someone's pimento cheese sandwich from the Masters. "When I started back in '97 with the logo, I just figured it was a great way to sell it. We've got a great relationship with Hooters. I help them and they help me this week. It's a good week. The money doesn't really matter to me. It's just so much fun to be out here, seeing people, getting the brand out."

It used to be a sad look when he first started doing this: Daly, with his incredible golf skills being wasted, peddling cheesy T-shirts and hats from a parking lot outside of Augusta National instead of bombing long drives down the fairways of Augusta National and competing for a green jacket.

Daly played in 12 Masters in his career and had one top-10 finish—a tie for third in 1993, his second try. He missed the cut in four of his final five Masters, including the last three, his final invite coming in 2006.

He's in his fifties now and is a part-time player on the Champions Tour, complaining of arthritis in his knees that prevents him from walking more than six or seven holes. So, this road show is pretty much his full-time gig. The Masters stop is the 11th in a 37-week tour that Daly has scheduled this year.

What once looked and felt like a sad small-town carnival act has become a wildly popular and profitable venture for Daly, who sets up shop at about 8:00 AM and is still selling and signing well past dinnertime.

You never know who's going to stop by and see Daly. Daly said Eric Trump was over the other day. Former Cowboys great defensive lineman Ed "Too Tall" Jones has visited, as has Cowboys head coach Jason Garrett.

Dave Saracino, a high-ranking executive with BIC (pens and lighters), befriended Daly years ago and visits him regularly.

"This says that he's us," Saracino said, looking around at the mob scene jockeying for position to get close to Daly. "There's nothing else you can say except he's the real deal. He's as great as he ever was. If he could putt, he'd win everything."

Hearing that backhanded compliment, Daly interjected, saying, "I can't putt? It ain't my putting, man. It's my attitude."

If you ask the masses who line up all day to see Daly as a folk hero, they have no problem with his attitude.

Cory Moore, a private security guard who travels with Daly in his RV, said, "I have a video of about 200 people chanting his name the night before last when he walked off the bus."

Moore stays around Daly's RV until about 3:30 in the morning every day to make sure people don't bother him late at night.

"I've found people knocking on the bus," Moore said. "They're just having fun. They're excited to see him, because nobody else comes and does this."

The only trouble that Daly has encountered with his Hooters setup came in 2018, when his RV was hit by a car. Daly said the RV was hit when a driver tried to make a U-turn but lost control of the car. He said he tweaked his knee while trying to get out of harm's way.

"It whaled into the front of the bus," his fiancée, Anna Cladakis, told GolfChannel.com. "John dove out of the way."

It's difficult to properly measure who loves who more: Daly or his fans.

"The greatest thing for me is when someone comes up and says, 'My son started playing golf because of you,' or, 'I started playing golf because of you,'" Daly said. "We're like family. It's the Hooters tradition. It's just awesome. We've got like 20,000 to 30,000 people coming through here."

Daly hopes to be at Hooters for as long as he can stand, an institution outside of the real institution in town. Augusta National, however, has been purchasing swaths of land along Washington Road with rumors of building another golf course and expanding its brand.

That land expansion project has been creeping its way down Washington Road toward Hooters, with rumors that the club eventually wants its own exit ramp off of Interstate 20 to expedite its patrons' arrival to the Masters.

That, of course, would be a crushing blow to the endless rows of businesses along Washington Road, which depend on that Masters traffic stopping at their stores. Hooters is one of those. Daly, however, doesn't believe the expansion is going to take over Hooters.

"From what I understand, I was told they did a 20-year lease and they put me in the lease," Daly said. "I doubt I'll be here by then—I'll be 73—but you never know. As long as they don't get mad at me for signing girls' asses, I'm okay."

The green jackets of Augusta National, as they do for a number of other places, have seemingly ignored Daly's sideshow...or at least looked the other way. Whether or not the club embraces it is an entirely different story.

"Hey, I've always had respect for the members and the guys in there," Daly said of Augusta National. "It's really been the only place where I haven't been in trouble."

Paul Azinger, who, like Daly, has sometimes been a bit irreverent compared to the general conservative golf establishment, said he didn't know "what to think" about the Daly show outside Augusta National when he first saw it.

"It just felt like John Daly being John Daly, renegade, building a brand," Azinger said. "He was a brand all unto his own because of his wild nature, that image with the mullet. It became pretty clear pretty quickly that he had a drinking problem and gambling problem and he was able to admit those. He's one of those obsessive compulsives. You have to be that way to play great golf, and he epitomized that.

"The one great thing Daly always had going for him was he didn't really have any secrets, which is a pretty nice way to live your life. Not having any secrets and being an open book to all who loved him, it made them love him more. He hit it a mile. He had all the ingredients to be super popular."

Azinger, though, still to this day wonders aloud how Daly didn't have more success inside the gates and ropes at Augusta.

"I thought Augusta was perfect for John Daly, as high as he hit it, as far as he hit it, and the way he putted," Azinger said. "He had a magnificent short game. But I don't even remember him contending there. I think he was having performance anxiety. There was a lot going on inside his head."

Chapter 16

LEFTY

Phil Mickelson had won 21 tournaments on the PGA Tour by the time he arrived at Augusta National in April of 2004 to play in his 11th career Masters as a pro.

As had become a personal tradition for Mickelson, he would collect the flag from the 18th green pin after every one of those wins and present it to his grandfather, Al Santos, as a keepsake.

Around Christmas of 2003, Al Santos told his grandson, half-joking but serious, too, "I don't want any more of these Tour wins; I want a major."

For all of his previous successes—far from a career to sneeze at—Mickelson had played in 46 major championships as a professional without winning one. And it was becoming a *thing* for Mickelson, whose failure to capture a major despite his enormous talent essentially spawned the label: "Best player never to win a major."

Mickelson—and his grandfather, too—was tired of hearing his name associated with that label.

So, he went and won that 2004 Masters, breaking his 0-for-46 streak in majors. Unfortunately, his grandfather wasn't around to witness it or receive the flag from the 18th hole of Augusta

National. He died at the age of 97 in January 2004, shortly after he spoke those motivational words to his grandson.

"He said to me around that Christmas before he passed, 'This is your year,'" Mickelson recalled right after he won. "As that winning putt caught the left lip and fell in, I couldn't help but think he may have had something to do with it."

There are a number of poignant, if spiritual, moments Mickelson remembered from that '04 Masters.

Moments before he left the house he had been renting to go play the most important round of golf of his life that Sunday morning of the final round, he looked at his wife, Amy, and said, "It feels different. It is different."

Heartbreak had become such a fabric of the Mickelson narrative in major championships. There was, for example, Payne Stewart seizing the moment from Mickelson at the 1999 U.S. Open at Pinehurst and David Toms doing the same thing at the 2001 PGA Championship. Both made putts on the final hole to beat Mickelson.

In that fateful final round in '04, it was Mickelson who seized every moment and exorcised every demon, carding birdies on five of the final seven holes to capture what would be the first of three green jackets he would win. He finished 9-under par overall and turned that final round into the most exhilarating final round since Jack Nicklaus won in 1986 at age 46.

Mickelson shot 31 on the back nine, the lowest total since Nicklaus shot 30 in 1986, and won it with an 18-foot downhill birdie putt on the 72nd hole.

He leaped into the air, with both arms and his putter raised to the sky, hugged caddie Jim "Bones" Mackay, and told him, "I did it!"

Finally, Mickelson was a major winner, a green jacket owner. The daredevil way Mickelson did it added to the thrill of victory.

He outdueled Ernie Els in a dazzling back nine that climaxed with a birdie on the 72nd and final hole to clinch the victory, only the fourth time in Masters history that had happened.

The exclamation point he put on the day was all Mickelson all the way in that it was an utter thrill ride to the end. The winning putt caught the left edge of the cup and spun tantalizingly around it before disappearing into the hole.

Mickelson marched immediately to his wife, Amy, lifted her in the air, and hugged her, and then he picked up his three-year-old daughter, Amanda, and said to her, "Daddy won. Can you believe it?"

Mickelson himself couldn't.

"This doesn't feel real," he said. "I can't believe this is happening."

He called it "an amazing day" and "a fulfillment of dreams," and said it was a moment "I'm going to relive in my mind forever and ever."

There were so many moments from which to choose for Mickelson on that magical day, beginning with the events leading up to that winning putt, with his playing partner and friend, Chris DiMarco, leaving his bunker shot two inches outside Mickelson's ball marker on the same line.

That DiMarco was going to have to give Mickelson a read on his eventual winning putt was one of those signs of fate that the fabled place simply offers up at the most poignant moments.

"Surreal," Mickelson called it.

"It was meant to be for him," DiMarco said afterward. "To be quite honest, I didn't think there was any way he would miss that putt. It was just time."

Mickelson said of the putt on 18, "The first thing went through my mind was my ball was on the same line that DiMarco missed from the same spot, and I thought I had missed it low.

But my ball rung around the cup and went in. And the first thing that went in my head was my grandfather nudged that ball in.

"We had that conversation before he passed away earlier that year, and he said to me, 'You're going to win the Masters this year.' So, in my head that was always what gave me that belief that this was my year. So, when that putt went in that conversation was the first thing that went on in my head."

Mickelson has never been short on confidence or the power of positive thinking. Every morning he wakes up optimistic about what's going to occur that day. He was on record long before 2004 in saying that he was going to win the Masters and he wasn't going to win just one major championship, he was going to win multiple majors.

He would go on to win the 2006 Masters and again in 2010. Those three Masters victories, coupled with the 2005 PGA Championship and 2013 British Open, give him five career majors, a mere U.S. Open victory short of an elusive and rare career Grand Slam, which only six players have accomplished.

"In '04, I had played so well at the start of the year and I had put in this extra time that I hadn't done in the past and I felt really prepared for that Masters," Mickelson said. "But you never know how it's going to play out. That front nine on Sunday just didn't go as I had planned."

He fixed that with the 31 on the back nine, which would vanquish a very good run by Ernie Els.

"It was when the putt went in on 12 that sparked the round," Mickelson said. "Ernie was ahead of me and he had already birdied 13. That putt on 12 was the big thing, because if I make that I'm really only one back and if that one doesn't go in then I've got a lot of ground to make up.

"When that putt on 12 went in, I knew I was going to birdie 13, because that hole sets up well for me. I hit a good drive and hit 7-iron so now I make birdie and I'm only one back with five holes to go. I didn't know where I was going to make up the ground but I felt I would."

When Mickelson failed to birdie the par-5 15th hole, it could have derailed his run.

"Not birdieing 15 was difficult, but I was playing so well it didn't bother me the way it normally would," he said. "Normally, I feel like I've got to birdie the par-5s, but I felt like I was playing so well that I would have chances the next three holes, which I ended up having.

"It was probably the most exciting moment in my career, to birdie the last hole to win by one. To win my first major, at the Masters, my favorite event, it was by far the most exciting moment of my career. The most fulfilling was winning the [2013] British Open, because I always knew I would win the Masters and I knew I would win it more than once. But the British Open? I didn't know if I would ever win that. So that first Masters was, by far, the greatest moment."

———

Witness to Final-Round Frenzy

Masters Sundays are, quite simply, as electric as they are unique to anything you'll ever experience if you're fortunate enough to witness one in person.

You don't need a TV or radio to keep you informed about what's going on around you. You can, instead, read the action based on the decibel level of the roars from particular holes and figure out exactly what's transpiring around the storied grounds. That 2004 Mickelson final round was the blueprint.

For example, as I walked toward Amen Corner to position myself to see the leaders come through the most fabled three holes in golf, a roar that more resembled a cheer for a game-winning touchdown in a football game emanated from the 11th hole.

As I waited to cross the 15th tee box, where Fred Couples was standing over his tee shot, the roars were so loud and sustained that Couples had to back off his shot three times. If you'd been to Augusta before, you knew this was not a birdie roar. It was an eagle roar—this one for a 220-yard K.J. Choi hole-out on the par-4 11th.

Once I arrived to Amen Corner and situated myself on a media grandstand that used to overlook the 11th, 12th, and 13th holes, I watched as Mickelson, one shot behind Els at the moment, stood over his birdie putt as the galleries at the 13th hole unleashed a roar so thunderous it could have been a game-winning Derek Jeter home run at Yankee Stadium.

It meant eagle for Els and a three-shot deficit for Mickelson, and Mickelson knew it. Still, he never backed off his putt and drained the must-make birdie to stay within two.

Once Mickelson putted out, I raced over to a grandstand on 15 that also overlooks the par-3 16th hole.

Just as I arrived there, Padraig Harrington delivered a hole-in-one on 16, leaving the massive crowds around that corner of the course delirious. Less than 10 minutes later, Kirk Triplett duplicated Harrington's feat and holed out on 16, falling to his back and lying on the tee box ground as the crowds erupted in disbelief.

At age 43 at the time and having played golf for some 20 years and watched it longer, I'd never seen a hole-in-one live. Suddenly, I'd seen two in less than 10 minutes.

A short time later, Els would march through and birdie No. 15 to get to 8-under-par while Mickelson was carding birdie on No. 13 to get to 6-under and the place was abuzz.

With Els approaching the 18th tee, Mickelson would then drain a 15-foot birdie putt on 16 to tie it at 8-under and the booming roar from there had those around the entire course in a state of bedlam, with fans racing to the 18th green to get a glimpse of the climax.

Els, who heard the sounds coming from 16 and knew exactly what it meant, called the noise "probably the loudest I've ever heard it."

It was never greater than when Mickelson, playing in the final group of the day and needing birdie to win, was on 18, where he delivered one of those signature Masters moments—the one that had eluded him through 10-plus frustrating near-miss years of no wins in majors—and it seemed you could hear the sounds from the crowd around 18, reverberating through the tall Georgia pines and all the way to Yankee Stadium in New York.

Shot of a Lifetime

Of the three Masters Mickelson has won, because of the way he executed his third victory at Augusta, none represented who he is more than the 2010 Masters.

All because of one shot. One memorable shot that will forever be a part of Masters lore as one of the greatest ever struck.

It was a 6-iron from a pine-straw lie behind two trees to the right of the par-5 13th fairway, 187 yards over Rae's Creek to the green and 207 yards to the flag that Mickelson pulled off that probably defines his career more than any shot he's ever made and any tournament he's ever won.

Mickelson had just birdied the 12th hole to take the tournament lead for the first time all week. And, as he arrived to the resting spot from his tee shot gone slightly errant, Mickelson took little time to assess his next strategic move.

"I'm going for it," he told his caddie, Jim "Bones" Mackay.

Mackay, who was known in his 25 years on Mickelson's bag as Mickelson's conscience, almost always wanted to err on the side of caution in moments like that. The two have had numerous back-and-forth conversations in the heat of battle about which shot to take, Mickelson always wanting to take the bold chance and Mackay always trying to rein him in.

Nothing was going to change Mickelson's mind on this shot, though.

Years later, recounting the shot and its magnitude, Mickelson said, "That was one of those moments, I remember having a conversation [with Mackay] as I was standing over the shot and being asked for the fourth time, 'Are you sure you want to do this?' And finally saying, 'Look, at some point you're going to have to make a great shot if you want to win.'

"And this was that moment. Sometimes you just have to clutch up and hit the shot and pull something off, pull off a tough shot. It wasn't a hard shot, but the penalty if I missed it was going to be severe. It was going to hit a tree or it was going to go into the water."

Mackay said the shot "was much scarier in person," adding, "The gap in the trees was much smaller than it looked like on TV. It was about the width of a box of a dozen balls I would say. The thing I was concerned about was there was a lot of pine straw and you could lose your footing. If you lose your footing, who knows where the ball is going to go?

"Phil let me know almost right away, 'I'm going for it here. When the green clears in front of us I'm going.'"

Mackay, trying to lay out every scenario to his man, reminded Mickelson, "Don't forget when you made all the eagles [in Saturday's third round] on 13, 14, and almost 15, don't forget that pitch shot you made.

"I was basically saying if it comes to you laying up here, you're as likely or more likely to get up and down and make four as anybody in the tournament," Mackay recalled. "He said, 'No, I'm absolutely going for this.' So, I backed off and waited for the green to clear."

As they waited, Mackay had gotten word from a TV person that K.J. Choi, who was playing in the group ahead, had just bogeyed the 13th hole to fall two strokes behind Mickelson, which prompted Mackay to say to Mickelson, "Hey, let me throw this at you. You're the boss, but does this change the way you're going to approach this shot given the fact that you are tied for the lead now?"

Mickelson's response is something that will be burned in Mackey's memory forever.

"He looked at me and said, 'Let me tell you something. If I am going to win this tournament today, I am going to have to hit a really good shot under a lot of pressure at some point. I am going to do it right now,'" Mackay recalled. "That was my entrée to get out of the way and watch him do his thing. And he hit arguably the greatest shot of his career. You almost knew he was going to hit a great shot based simply on the way he said what he said."

What does Mackay remember most about the actual shot?

"The great thing about that shot for me was the sound," he said. "The second he hit it, he hit it so pure that we knew it was going to carry."

Nick Faldo told CBS viewers, "That was the greatest shot of his life."

Mickelson, always as much a scientist as a swashbuckler, explained, "That year I did a lot of blind testing with Dave Pelz [a short game guru] to try to get my swing grooved and not see where the ball goes so that you don't make adjustments. You get every club dialed in. Well, I couldn't see that shot. Even though from behind the ball you could see the pin, standing where a left hander was standing all I saw was a tree trunk. And it took me right back to that blind test where it said, 'Trust your swing. Just make a good swing. I know this 6-iron goes straight, just make a good swing.' That's all I tried to do.

"I think that's what happens in majors. You have to go back to your practice sessions to get you through it. And that was the one...at the highest stage, too."

Mickelson would later joke with reporters after his victory that "the gap [between the trees] wasn't huge, but it was big enough, you know, for a ball to fit through."

When a reporter asked Mickelson to explain the difference between a "great shot" and a "smart shot," he said, "A great shot is when you pull it off. A smart shot is when you don't have the guts to try it."

That sentiment surprised no one close to Mickelson.

"That's him; that's how he's built," Mackay said. "He plays completely without fear. He's absolutely convinced he can pull off every shot. He wouldn't want to play any other way."

Steve Loy, Mickelson's former college coach at Arizona State and longtime manager, echoed Mackay's sentiments, saying, "That's Phil. The weaker players are always utilizing that kind of thinking as, 'I'm not going to beat myself.' He'd rather be bold enough to have the courage to do what most people can't."

Lee Westwood, who was Mickelson's playing partner in that final round, marveled at what he saw.

"It's really one of the few shots that only Phil could pull off," Westwood said. "It was a high-tariff shot. I think most people would have just chipped that one out. But, you know, that's what great players do—pull off great shots at the right time. I knew that he fancied having a go at it and that's Phil's personality and game. He's that kind of player. That's what everybody wants to see. That's why everybody likes watching him."

Mickelson didn't drain the short eagle putt, but he settled for birdie on 13 and he followed that with two more birdies on the final six holes and won by three shots.

"His life changed when he made the putt on 18 at Augusta in 2004," Mackay said of Mickelson's first Masters victory. "But [the shot at 13] was the best shot I've ever seen him hit."

When it was all over and Mickelson, showered with cheers from the packed gallery, walked off the 18th hole, he spotted his wife, Amy, who had been battling breast cancer. The medications she was on had weakened her to the point where he was not sure she'd be able to get to Augusta.

They embraced for what seemed like an eternity as the golf world looked on with tears.

"It had been an emotional year, and I was very proud of her fight and struggle she'd been through, and to come out on top in that tournament was very emotional," Mickelson said. "I don't normally shed tears over wins, and when Amy and I hugged off 18 that was a very emotional moment for us and something that I'll look back on and just cherish.

"She came in for the weekend. It was not even quite a year [since the diagnosis], but we had gotten through some of the worst stuff and that was the most emotional because of all the things we had been going through. Golf, being able to play and be on a golf course, was kind a reprieve from some of the stuff that was going on. It was more relaxing for me, and I ended up playing well that week."

———

The Forgotten Green Jacket

Because of the drama associated with Mickelson's 2004 win, his first major championship victory, and his 2010 win, defined by that shot on 13, his 2006 Masters win is probably the least memorable of the three—the proverbial middle child.

But it happened to come in the middle of perhaps the hottest playing stretch of his career. That '06 Masters was Mickelson's third major championship victory in nine starts, and second in a row after having won the 2005 PGA Championship. In fact, he fell just short in that final-hole collapse at Winged Foot in 2006 of capturing three consecutive majors.

Mickelson, with four birdies in his final-round 69, won that Masters by two shots over Tim Clark, who holed out from the right bunker on the 72nd hole.

Five players—Tiger Woods, two-time Masters winner José María Olazábal, Retief Goosen, Fred Couples, and Chad Campbell—tied for third place, three shots behind Mickelson.

"When I look back on it, I think what I'm most proud of is that I didn't let other people back in it," Mickelson said. "They had to come and chase me down and make birdies to do it."

Mickelson had come into that '06 Masters on a tear, a week removed from winning the BellSouth Classic in Atlanta by 13 shots at 28-under par.

"The only year that I really knew going in that I was most likely going to win was in '06, because I had just won by 13 the week before and I felt like I was playing so good that if I just carried anywhere near close to that level I was going to have a good week," Mickelson said. "When I won in '04, I always knew I would win, but I never knew when it was going to happen. I had a good feeling about that week in the sense that I just kind of believed that I was going to win, but I didn't know it the way I knew it in '06.

"I had a good feeling about that tournament, I knew I was playing well, I knew I was prepared, but I still had to execute."

With Augusta lengthening the golf course 155 yards for that 2006 Masters, Mickelson went with the unconventional strategy of using two drivers that year—one for a draw and the other for a fade—and he ended up leading the field in average driving distance.

"It was a huge help," Mickelson recalled. "I got 20, 25 more yards with the driver that draws."

He'd experimented with the two drivers the week before in Atlanta and it worked out well.

"I'd like to say one thing about the changes," Mickelson, ever the tinkerer, said. "I like them."

A big edge for Mickelson in the final round was that his playing partner was Couples, one of his good friends in the game. That proved to be a highly advantageous pairing for him.

"I love playing with Fred," Mickelson said. "We had a great time and we kept saying how lucky we were to be in the final pairing on Sunday at the Masters, and how much fun it was. It made for a very fun day. We were pulling for each other to make some birdies and encouraging each other. I felt this great feeling of accomplishment to be able to beat guys like Tiger and Retief and Ernie [Els] and Vijay [Singh] and Fred and some incredible and talented players."

After taking a one-shot lead into that final round, Mickelson carried a three-shot lead up the 18th fairway and reveled in the "stress-free" walk.

———

Spikegate

For all the pleasant memorable experiences Mickelson has had at Augusta, there was one that took place in the 2005 tournament that he'd rather forget: some contentious moments with Vijay Singh, who'd complained in the middle of the second round that the spikes in Mickelson's golf shoes were leaving marks on the greens.

Singh sent a rules official to Mickelson's group in the middle of the round to measure Mickelson's spikes, infuriating the usually affable Mickelson.

That led to an explosive incident that escalated into an animated shouting match between Mickelson and Singh when they bumped into each other in the Champions Locker Room during a weather delay later on.

Singh, the No. 1 player in the world at the time, delivered what one player called "a completely classless" move of "clear gamesmanship" when he complained to a Masters referee about Mickelson's spikes during the Friday completion of the first round.

Singh, playing in the group behind Mickelson, summoned a referee at the 12th hole, where he was playing at the time, and complained that Mickelson's spikes were leaving large spike marks in the green.

"He said on the 12th hole that someone in the group in front was tracking the green with his shoes," PGA Tour rules official Steve Rintoul said. "When he looked at where the track was going, he figured out it was Phil."

Mickelson hit his tee shot down the left side of the 13th fairway, and a rules official met him off the tee. Mickelson showed him his soles, one then the other. Rintoul said another official on the 13th green watched for abnormal footprints and found there was no problem.

According to Joe Damiano, the caddie for Stuart Appleby, Mickelson's playing partner in the round, the referee told Mickelson another official was going to be sent out to "file down" his spikes, causing Appleby to crack, "What are they going to send? A blacksmith?"

The official with a file was never sent out and Mickelson continued playing in his own size 12 Callaway shoes.

According to Damiano, Mickelson remained outwardly calm about the odd inquiry as he played out his first round. But, Damiano said the Singh complaint infuriated Mickelson, the defending Masters champion.

Mickelson later walked into the locker room and saw Singh sitting at a table with fellow player Mark O'Meara, and said Singh asked if he'd like Mickelson to take him outside and "kick his ass."

Mickelson, trying to downplay the incident, said, "I was extremely distracted and would have appreciated if it would have been handled differently or after the round. After sitting in the locker room for a while, I heard Vijay talking to other players about it and I confronted him. He expressed his concerns. I expressed my disappointment with the way it was handled.

"Given the wet and slippery conditions, more than a third of the field is using steel spikes. And I make every effort to tap down whatever spike marks I leave."

Mickelson was wearing metal eight-millimeter spikes in his golf shoes, which is commonplace, though many players had gone to plastic soft spikes by then.

Appleby was shocked by Singh, saying, "You never do something like that in the middle of a round. That's something you take up with the player after the round is over."

He also chided Singh, the 2001 Masters champion, for not having the "guts" to speak to Mickelson one-to-one about the issue.

He suggested Singh, who was 2-under at the time and just coming off a bogey at No. 11, recognized Mickelson, who was 3-under at the time, was playing well so he was obviously trying to throw him off his game.

According to Will Nicholson, the chairman of the Masters competition committee, there was "no ruling" and Mickelson's spikes were within the rules.

"We got a call, and how it got labeled onto Phil I have no idea," Nicholson said. "There was some spike that apparently tore up some grass, and Phil was the one that was blamed. One of our officials talked to Phil to see if there was a burr on the side of one of his spikes. He very generously, as you know he would, said he would change them if there was a problem. There wasn't."

Of course, in Sunday's final round, Mickelson and Singh were paired together in a tension-packed twosome. Not surprisingly, neither played well as Tiger Woods went on to win his fourth green jacket.

Singh finished one stroke better than Mickelson, whose 74 included double bogeys on the par-3 12th and 16th holes that ended his quest to win back-to-back Masters.

After the round, Singh refused to address the Spikegate incident and Mickelson refused to blame his poor performance on the distraction of the unfortunate pairing.

"That stuff was not a factor at all," Mickelson said.

Then, almost tongue-in-cheek, Mickelson said of himself and Singh, "We had a great day. We had a great time. We laughed. We giggled. We had a great time. It was a fun day."

For sure, he'd had better days at the Masters, and there, too, were more to come.

PART SIX

SATURDAY

Chapter 17

THE GREEN JACKET

It's not the most fashionable garment you've ever seen. It's not even worth that much money, believed to be valued at about $250. It's just a green jacket. And who wears green jackets, anyway?

Augusta National members do. So do Masters champions.

The green jacket is to golf what the Lombardi Trophy is to the NFL or the Stanley Cup is to the NHL. It's the pinnacle of awards for golfers, the most iconic trophy in the sport.

The Pantone 342–colored green jacket was first awarded to Masters winners in 1949, the 15th Masters. Augusta National members were the first to wear the green jacket; it was introduced as a means for members of the public to spot them amongst the crowd during tournament week.

Bobby Jones, the co-designer of Augusta National, attended a dinner at Royal Liverpool Golf Club where club captains were all wearing matching club jackets. That's where the idea of the green jackets was born.

The first were bought from Brooks Uniform Company in New York, but the members found them to be uncomfortable, made of too-thick material.

Since 1967, the jackets have been made by Hamilton Tailoring Company out of Cincinnati, with the tropical-weight wool material sourced from Dublin, Georgia. The brass buttons are made in Massachusetts. The breast-pocket patch, with the club's logo, is sewn in North Carolina.

The jacket belonging to the winner of the first ever tournament, Horton Smith in 1934, was sold at auction by family members for $600,000.

Each Masters winner is given a jacket. Regardless of how many Masters they've won, though, they have one jacket, and it resides in their locker at the club. For example, Jack Nicklaus has won a record six Masters, but he doesn't have six green jackets.

Green jacket holders are forbidden from taking them from the grounds of Augusta National. The only exception is the current winner, and he can only have it off the premises for the year after he's won it.

Tournament winners are given a temporary jacket when they win before having a customized fit delivered in the weeks following their victory. Then they're required to return it to the club upon their return to defend the title.

Gary Player is the only player to have broken the rule. After his 1961 win, Player returned from South Africa with his green jacket and then lost in a playoff to Arnold Palmer in 1962 and went back home with it to South Africa.

"I win the tournament and I assume when they put the jacket on you, that's your jacket," Player said. "I'm so excited; I leave and I go home to South Africa with the jacket. Three days later, I hear this call, 'Gary, this is Clifford Roberts here.' I said, 'I hope you're not calling me reverse charges,' because you know, you had to make him laugh a little bit because he was quite a dour man. He said, 'I believe, Gary, you've taken the jacket home to South Africa.'

"I said, 'I did, Mr. Roberts.' He said, 'Nobody ever takes the jacket off these grounds whatsoever.' So, I thought very quickly, and I said, 'Mr. Roberts, if you want it, come and fetch it.' He saw the lighter side of things and he said, 'Please don't ever wear it in public.'

"It's not like today. If you win today, you can wear it in public for one year. That didn't apply then. I put a plastic cover over it and never used it again until I came back."

Nicklaus joked, "Can you imagine in those days Clifford Roberts going to South Africa to fetch Gary's jacket?"

"Only a 40-hour flight in those days with no jets," Player joked.

Tom Watson recalled the first time he won the Masters, in 1977, the jacket he received wasn't his size of 42 regular. Augusta National usually sizes up potential champions, but instead gave him a 46 long. "They didn't assess my size very well," Watson said. "It didn't matter to me."

Nicklaus, too, had a size snafu. His first was a 46 long and his size is 43 regular.

"The next year when I came back, they didn't ask me to go get a jacket, never mentioned my jacket," Nicklaus recalled. "Tom Dewey had a jacket, former governor who lost to Truman in the presidency. His jacket fit me, and I wore his jacket for probably 15 years, maybe longer. Nobody ever mentioned, 'Do you have your green jacket?' I had Tom Dewey's. I never got a green jacket. Finally, I won six Masters and still nobody had ever given me a green jacket.

"I told the story to [then club chairman] Jack Stephens in 1998 and Jack Stephens said, 'What? You've never been given a green jacket?' I said, 'No. Nobody's ever mentioned it.' So, I got back the week of the tournament and he says, 'You will go down to the pro shop and you will be fit for your green jacket,' which is the one I wear now."

Tiger Woods, writing about his 1997 Masters win in his book *Unprecedented: The Masters and Me*, recalled: "After much celebration, I fell asleep fully clothed and hugging the green jacket like a blanket."

Over the years, some players have had some fun with the jacket in their year as champion. Sergio García, the 2017 winner, seemingly wore it every place he went.

"If I told you everywhere I took it, I will probably miss my tee time on Thursday," García joked when he returned to Augusta in 2018.

The most important place García wore the jacket was at his wedding to Angela Akins three months after his victory.

He also wore it to the "El Clasico" soccer match between Real Madrid and Barcelona, to Wimbledon for a Rafael Nadal match, to the New York Stock Exchange, and to numerous television studios for numerous guest appearances.

At one of the TV appearances, he hugged a stagehand who apparently had oil or grease on his shirt, which stained the jacket. "I'm thinking, 'My God, I've had the jacket for a day-and-a-half and I already have two massive stains on it,'" García recalled, saying he took it to a dry cleaner. "I think people know I've worn it and I don't like to show off and wear it left and right. At the end of the day, you've got to respect how iconic the jacket is. It's not just a piece of clothing. It means so much more than that. You have to be very respectful of it and wear it when you should, not all the time."

Jordan Spieth, the 2015 winner, recalled the feeling he had once he realized the jacket was his to wear for the year.

"It's once you leave the property, that's when it really hits you," Spieth said. "When you stand on the green it's one thing, but you're kind of thinking about what you want to say and how you want to thank everybody who made it possible. It's not until I left the property that I truly kind of felt what it was like to wear the jacket, and wear the jacket I did, for a year. It didn't leave my side."

Phil Mickelson was photographed wearing the jacket to a Krispy Kreme doughnut drive-thru in 2010. He, too, once joked that he would put the jacket in his golf bag and pull it out if it was chilly on the course.

Three-time winner Mickelson, ever the needler and practical jokester to friends, said, "I wouldn't carry three jackets around with me but I would say, 'I've got two more, if you're cold as well.'"

Patrick Reed, the 2018 winner, was asked about his favorite memory with the jacket.

"It would have had to have been right after we won and right after I got done talking in the press conference, right after we finished," he recalled. "I went back to Butler Cabin, and my daughter was there, and she just came over and gave me a big hug and told me I did it and told me she loved me. That is by far the best experience I've ever had with the green jacket.

"That's a memory and a moment that I'll never forget, no matter if I were to win multiple other green jackets. It's going to be hard to be able to top a moment like that that I was able to cherish with the little one."

He did have a funny exchange while wearing the jacket to a Knicks game at Madison Square Garden.

"It was on a Monday night, [my wife] Justine and I were at the Knicks game and were sitting courtside for the first time," Reed recalled. "I had Chris Rock right next to us. A couple seats down is 2 Chainz. He just kind of keeps looking down, and you can tell he's kind of looking down like, 'All right, this isn't the normal guy that sits in these seats; who is that?'

"And then when they announced me during one of the time-outs, then a couple minutes later there was a timeout and he just kind of reaches over, and he kind of touches the jacket, and he goes, 'So that's the real thing, huh?' I'm like, 'Yes, sir, yes, it is.' It's pretty cool to see just kind of the wide variety of people no matter what their background is, no matter what their age is or anything, how many people recognize the green jacket. I just think it's such a cool thing how many people recognize what the green jacket is and what it actually stands for."

Chapter 18

THE EL NIÑO ENIGMA

Sergio García, after he shot a disappointing 75 in the third round of the 2012 Masters (in which he would finish tied for 12th), sounded a bit dead inside.

In a shocking interview with Spanish reporters, García delivered a dark analysis of his state of mind as it related to winning a major championship, something he hadn't yet accomplished.

"I'm not good enough," García said. "I don't have the thing I need to have."

When asked if he meant winning the Masters, García said, "Any major."

"In 13 years, I have come to the conclusion that I need to play for second or third place," he said. "I'm not good enough, and today I know it. I've been trying for 13 years, and I don't feel capable of winning. I don't know what happened to me. Maybe it's something psychological. I'm not good enough for the majors.

"Tell me something I can do. I had my chances and opportunities and I wasted them. I have no more options. I wasted my options."

The day after that rant, García did not back off his comments.

"Everything I say, I say it because I feel it," García said. "If I didn't mean it, I couldn't stand here and lie like a lot of the guys do. If I felt like I could win, I would do it."

Three years before his 2012 self-loathing rant to the Spanish media, García, in an interview with the Golf Channel, torched Augusta National after his final-round 74 that left him tied for 38th in 2009.

"I don't like it, to tell you the truth," García said. "I don't think it's fair. It's too tricky. Even when it's dry, you still get mud balls in the middle of the fairway. It's just too much of a guessing game."

When he was asked how he would change Augusta National, García said, "I don't care. They can do whatever. It is not my problem. I just come here, play golf, and go home."

Two days later, García's management company did its best to quell the storm he created, releasing a damage-control statement supposedly from García. It read: "Out of frustration, I blamed the golf course instead of putting the blame where it belongs, on myself. Augusta National is one of the most iconic golf courses in the game and playing in the Masters each year is an honor."

———

Finally, a Breakthrough

It's weird how things turn out sometimes in sports.

After years of heartbreak (and a lot of bellyaching), García, a tortured soul of sorts in major championships, finally would win one. And at Augusta National, of all places.

He'd played in 73 career major championships, 71 of them consecutively, and posted top-10 finishes in nearly a third of them, with four second places. And finally, in 2017, García won a green jacket.

Five years earlier, after yet another disappointing Masters finish, García left everyone to believe he never would win a major because he said as much, conceding he felt like he simply didn't have it in him.

And yet, there was García in the final round of the 81st Masters, putting an end to all the doubt and all the pent-up frustration, winning at the place he had grown to loathe.

García, at age 37, was a major championship winner at last, overcoming years of baggage, doubt, jangled nerves, and, ultimately, Justin Rose on the first playoff hole, a birdie on 18 the difference.

"It's been such a long time coming," an emotional García said afterward. "There's always uncertainty. But, I felt a calmness I've never felt in a major championship Sunday."

There were signs all that week that suggested it might be a different tournament for García, one that would be special.

There was a poignant Wednesday night text message from fellow Spaniard and two-time Masters winner José María Olazábal imploring him to believe in himself that buoyed García's psyche.

There was the ball he hit on the 13th hole in the third round that somehow defied gravity and clung to the steep greenside bank instead of tumbling back into Rae's Creek. He converted what would have been an almost-certain bogey into a birdie. A lucky break for García, who has spent most of his career lamenting all the bad breaks he has endured.

Then there was No. 13 in the final round, when García pulled his drive into the trees and azaleas to the left of the fairway into an unplayable lie, forcing him to take a drop and penalty shot. He already was two shots behind Rose, his chances to win on life support.

But García somehow saved par with a punch shot from the pine needles to the fairway, a wedge onto the green and one putt, while Rose missed a five-foot birdie putt that could have given him a three-shot lead.

"Funny enough, most other weeks I would have been thinking, 'Here we go again,'" García said. "Obviously, I wasn't happy. But from there, the most important thing was that I felt calm. That calmness gave me confidence. I was like: 'It's okay. You're doing everything right. You're playing great. It's your time.' I just kept believing."

Then there was García carding an eagle on the par-5 15th hole to tie Rose at 9-under. The last Masters champion to make eagle on No. 15 en route to victory? Olazábal in 1994.

Good omens were everywhere for a change for García, who has spent his life playing the victim.

And finally, there was this: the Sunday of that final round would have been the 60th birthday of Seve Ballesteros, García's lifelong idol.

The ending was awkward, and it provided a perfect canvas for García to end his major championship drought. His weakness always has been his putting, and he failed to win the tournament on the 18th hole in regulation, missing a five-foot putt for the victory, leaving it right all the way, the ball never even grazing the cup.

In 2007, García lipped out an eight-foot putt for the win on the 72nd hole of the British Open, leading to a playoff he lost to Padraig Harrington.

His miss on 18 in the final round sent García and Rose back to the 18th tee for the playoff hole that García won thanks to Rose hitting his drive into the trees to the right of the fairway.

Rose, the 2013 U.S. Open winner and a friend of García's, understandably was gutted afterward, but was gracious in defeat. "If there was anyone to lose to, it would be Sergio," he said.

"He's had his fair share of heartbreak. It's nice for him now to have that monkey off his back, and I was very pleased for him."

To illustrate how far gone García's belief had gotten, you needed only to go back to those words after that 2012 Masters when asked if he thought he ever would win a major.

So much for that. A Masters hater had become a lover of Augusta National over the course of those four magical days in April 2017.

How did it happen?

Perhaps not without García meeting—and marrying—Angela Akins, who, by the accounts of those who know García well and other close observers, imbued him with a sense of belief.

"Angela is a good woman," said Danny Willett, the 2016 Masters champion who had the honor of slipping the green jacket over García's shoulders. "He has had a lot of years of heartache on the course and a little bit off it and he has found someone there who he loves and enjoys. It does make a difference. To have the stability off the course, it definitely does help you on the course."

Irishman and former Ryder Cup teammate Padraig Harrington said, "It's Angela who has been a big difference to him. I saw it in the team room at the last Ryder Cup (in 2016). When he holed the winning putt, she didn't come running on to the green. She waited to let him enjoy it. She is the big driving force."

Fellow Irishman Paul McGinley said he thinks Akins "has added the extra vital dimension" for García, adding, "It's not like he was miles away; he was just one percent away from being a major champion. She has that bit of steeliness about her, and I think that has permeated through to Sergio. There is a good team behind him, a real belief, and with the monkey off his back I wouldn't be surprised if it led to major number two, three, or even four."

Akins' father, Marty, is a former All-American college quarterback, and her grandfather was Ray Akins, a legendary high school football coach who was also the grandfather of New Orleans Saints quarterback Drew Bees. So there's some athletic strength in her family—strength that has seemingly permeated into García's competitive soul.

"They've definitely helped, there's no doubt the whole family has," García said after his Masters win. "Marty is a very, very positive, very, you know, outspoken and a very, very confident kind of guy. Angela is the same way. They are all very competitive.

"It's quite simple: when good people are telling you things you need to get better at, and they are telling you from their hearts, you listen, and that's what I did. Sometimes they tell me things I don't want to hear and it's not easy, because I know how much of a hard-headed man I can be. But it's been great.

"I didn't think I would be able to change this quickly, but I'm glad I did. It turned out to be an amazing week in a place I love but where I've had some tough times. To be able to deal with those emotions and accept the good and bad things was something that definitely gives me a sense of extra pride."

García credited his support system for helping carry him through some stressful moments in the final round of that '17 Masters—like when he bogeyed the 10th and 11th and then drove his tee shot into the trees at the par-five 13th.

"I was very calm, much calmer than I've felt in probably any major championship on Sunday," García said. "In the past at 13, I would have said to my caddie, 'Why doesn't it go through?' But I was like, 'If that's what's supposed to happen, let it happen. Let's try to make a great 5 here and see if we can put in a hell of a finish to have a chance.'"

García recalled a moment after one of his several disappointments at Augusta when 2009 Masters champion Ángel Cabrera offered him words of encouragement.

"Cabrera and I, we get along nicely, [and] he just kind of put his arm around me and said, 'You know, just keep going, don't worry about it, these things happen. If you keep going the way you're going, you'll be fine. You'll manage to get through one day.'"

———

No Defense

García's defense of the green jacket he won in 2017 is not so memorable. He finished in a tie for last place, oddly enough, with Willett, the 2016 champion.

What made García's 2018 Masters memorable for all the wrong reasons was *how* he flamed out in his title defense. He hit his five balls in the water on the par-5 15th hole en route to shooting an opening-round 81.

He took a 13 on the hole, ballooning his score at the time from 2-over-par to 10-over. His 13 tied Tommy Nakajima (1978, hole No. 15) and Tom Weiskopf (1980, No. 12) as the highest individual score on a hole in Masters history. Amazingly, García sank a nine-foot putt to avoid the 14 to own the record for highest score ever himself.

"It's the first time in my career where I make a 13 without missing a shot, simple as that," García said. "I felt like I hit a lot of good shots, and unfortunately the ball just didn't want to stop."

García's 81 was followed by a second-round 78 and an early-exit missed cut—though he had to stick around for the weekend to slip the green jacket over the next winner's shoulders, as is a part of the annual Masters ceremony.

"I'm disappointed and I would have loved to have had a better defense of my title," García said. "Unfortunately, this is golf, and sometimes that's what happens."

García, who named his daughter Azalea Adele in honor of his Masters victory and an ode to the name of the 13th hole at Augusta National, tweeted the day after his nightmare on No. 15 that year: "What happened on 15 yesterday was unfortunate for me and it hurt but I tried to handle it like a Masters champion should. That same hole gave me that green jacket last year so we might end up naming our next kid Firethorn.

Firethorn is the name of Augusta's 15th hole, which swallowed those five balls of García's and doomed him to the highest two-round total (159) ever posted by a defending Masters champion. It's also the hole where García hit an 8-iron that clipped the flag and set up a 12-foot eagle putt to tie him for the lead en route to his Masters victory the year before.

His week as defending champion was hardly the week García was expecting.

"I've talked to José María [Olazábal], and he told me when you get there and you go through the gates and drive down Magnolia Lane as a Masters champion...he couldn't explain the feeling, but he said, 'You'll just see it feels different,'" García said. "To walk around the grounds at Augusta and wearing the jacket and being seen as Masters champion and everything...it's just so different."

García's year following his Masters victory had been storybook. He married Akins and they had their daughter.

"I feel very proud for being able to win a major, and to win the Masters on top of that," García said. "But you know, like what they all tell me: 'Has it changed your life?' I don't think and I don't feel like it has. I'm still doing the same things. It's something that until it happens, you don't know what it's going to feel like and what it's going to do to you. But on my regard, I'm happy that I don't feel it has changed me. I don't feel like I'm better than I was before."

Akins, whom García met when she was working at the Golf Channel, has served as a massive positive force in his life.

"I remember a year before the [2017] Masters, being at Augusta with Sergio and talking about particular things that I thought he should work on," Akins recalled in 2018. "I remember he was talking about how somebody had gotten lucky and he had gotten unlucky. We talked about how you can't control that. You're just wasting your energy. He's gotten so much better than that. In golf, you get bad breaks all the time. And you get good breaks."

Chapter 19

THE BIG EASY

The list isn't a long one, but there have been a fair number of players who never fell in love with Augusta National and the Masters over the years.

One of the most prominent of those was Ernie Els, the affable South African, who had several near-misses trying to win a green jacket in his 23 attempts without reward and finally left with a bad taste in his mouth. Els had two runner-up finishes, edged out by Tiger Woods in 2000 and Phil Mickelson in 2004. In all, he posted six finishes in the top 8.

Before the 2019 Masters, which he had not qualified for, Els was resigned to the fact that he'd never get to play a 24th Masters and considered the venerable tournament dead to him.

"To be honest with you, I won't miss the place," Els said. "I had enough of it—especially the last five years I played it terribly."

Els' most recent results at Augusta at that time were, indeed, dodgy. He'd finished 53rd in 2017 after shooting 83–78 on the weekend. In 2016, he missed the cut after shooting 80–73. He had a missed cut in 2014 sandwiched between a tie for 22nd in 2015 and a tie for 13th in 2013. In 2012, he didn't even qualify to get into the field.

Els' theory is simply that some players at Augusta have been treated better by the golf gods than others.

"You can be on that curve—and I think Mickelson and Tiger and Freddie [Couples] are on that curve—and then you have me and [Tom] Weiskopf and [Greg] Norman on the other curve," Els said.

Mickelson, Woods, and Couples, who got that famous break in 1992 en route to winning when his ball somehow stayed on the grassy bank at No. 12 and didn't trickle into Rae's Creek in the final round, always seem to have had positive memories at Augusta.

Els—like Norman and Weiskopf, who also never won despite heartbreaking close calls—not so much.

"When a thing stings you it keeps stinging you," Els said. "When it gives to you it keeps on giving. I've seen that with Gary Player. I've seen it with Jack [Nicklaus]. I've got a love-hate relationship with the place. It was always almost like a curse to me. It was not a romantic deal to me. It was a fucking nightmare for the most part.

"Then," Els went on, "you start disliking the place when you shouldn't. I try to keep my honor for the golf course and the people, because the members are great and the course is actually great. But it just doesn't want to give me anything and then I was finally like, 'You know what? That's fine. Let's move on.'

"It's like, 'Shit, it's not giving me anything. How many times do you want to run into a wall?' That's how I felt my last couple of years. I didn't want to say it before, and I don't have any bad feelings about it. It's just the way it is. I had enough of it. Move on. It's a unique place, but I'm done with it. It's done with me."

The shame of this is that Els had some brilliant runs at the green jacket. He lost to Mickelson in one of the most epic Sunday back-nine duels in tournament history. His final-round 67 wasn't enough as Mickelson shot 30 on the back nine and won his first career major.

"I don't really have any Masters highlights," Els said. "I guess the final round in '04 was a highlight. I'm just glad that I had the experience that Nicklaus and Phil and Tiger and all the great Masters players had in that I was in the mix once, I mean really in the heat of it. That Sunday was phenomenal. It was one of the best ever. It was obviously a huge disappointment to me, but when I look back now, at least I can say that I was in the mix when the crowds were going nuts. I was hitting good shots and my opponents are hitting good shots."

Els' most embarrassing moment came in 2016, when he took a record nine on the first hole in the opening round. En route to that stunning number, Els six-putted from two feet.

"I can't explain it," Els said after shooting 80 that day. "It's unexplainable. I couldn't get the putter back. I was standing there and I've got a three-footer. I've made thousands of three-footers. And I just couldn't take it back. And then I just kind of lost count. I tried to fight. I don't know how I stayed out there [and finished]."

Els, who'd been battling the putting yips at that time in his career, made a reference to having "snakes" in his head.

"It's the first time ever I've seen anything like that," Jason Day, Els' playing partner for those first two rounds, said. "I feel for Ernie. I've known Ernie for a long time now. I didn't realize he was fighting stuff like that upstairs with the putter. You just don't want to see any player go through that."

The quintuple-bogey is the highest score on the first hole in Masters history, surpassing the 8s taken by Olin Browne and Scott Simpson in 1998, Billy Casper in 2001, and Jeev Milkha Singh in 2007.

Tom Watson once 5-putted the 16th green at Augusta. Seve Ballesteros is famous for his quote following a 4-putt at a Masters years ago. When he was asked to describe how he 4-putted, he said, "I miss, I miss, I miss, I make."

As a credit to Els, he powered on and didn't quit the round, something the likes of John Daly might have done.

"I don't know how I stayed out there," he said. "But you love the game and you've got to have respect for the tournament and so forth. The last thing you want to do is do that on a golf course."

The next day, Els said he walked to the practice range to warm up for the second round and could see pity in people's faces.

"It was a very weird, surreal feeling," said Els, who shot 73 in the second round and missed the cut. "I walked on to the range and even the players and caddies, they kind of just looked at me as if I don't have pants on or something, or like I stole something. But they've got a good reason to look at me funny for what happened. [That first hole] was just absolutely nightmarish. After what I did you feel quite embarrassed."

Els' odd meltdown was reminiscent of some athletes in other sports who had their own form of the yips.

Former New York Mets catcher Mackey Sasser was once unable to throw the ball back to the pitcher without pumping his fist into his glove several times. That led to base runners stealing bases in bunches, leading to Sasser eventually having to quit the game.

Former New York Yankees second baseman Chuck Knoblauch, in the '90s, lost his ability to throw to first base. Knoblauch, once a Gold Glove fielder, lost his career to the weird affliction.

St. Louis Cardinals pitcher Rick Ankiel suffered a mental and physical meltdown in the 2000 playoffs, throwing a series of wild pitches. It affected him so profoundly that he was never able to find the strike zone again and had to quit pitching. Ankiel went to the minor leagues and tried to make it as an outfielder.

Returning to golf, Tiger Woods went through the chipping yips, seemingly related to his back ailments. It led to a stunning 82 in the second round of the 2015 Waste Management Phoenix Open.

If Woods, arguably the greatest golfer ever, can get the yips, then nobody is immune.

Els was warmed by the reaction he got from the spectators in the wake of his nightmare.

"The patrons were great toward me," he said. "I appreciate that. You play long enough, you make a fool of yourself somewhere, but I did it on the biggest stage. But I'll take something out of this. I'll sit down and see where we go."

Els said he'd been "working on something" with his short putting stroke that "backfired" on that opening hole.

"I was trying some new stuff—can you believe it?—from Tuesday onwards [and] I thought it might be something in the right direction, but obviously it wasn't," he said. "Maybe I felt like that because my brain [was] telling me, 'This is not normal' and [it] just went haywire."

Els said he went back to his rented house the night after the first round. "I think we were all still in shock, the whole household. We just weren't saying much, and I had my dinner and watched the NBA game, Miami against Chicago. Just kind of shell-shocked. I slept okay, and then [Friday] morning I felt very bad when I got to the course. You feel weird. People kind of give you a funny look, not the normal look. I was feeling down, really down. I felt kind of embarrassed. I didn't feel like myself."

Perhaps the most poignant moment of the entire affair came after Els' first round. *Augusta Chronicle* golf writer Scott Michaux bumped into Els in the clubhouse grill and asked him, "How you holding up?"

"I'm a little dead inside," Els responded.

Chapter 20

THE PROTEST

Martha Burk doesn't play golf. She never had any ambition to become a member of Augusta National.

But she'll go down as one of the most influential figures in the history of Augusta National in that she helped open the club's doors to female members.

It was a well-publicized campaign in 2002 and 2003 to get the most exclusive golf club on the planet to invite women into its membership orchestrated by Burk, a leader of the National Council of Women's Organizations, that helped elicit change.

Burk waged a very public battle with William "Hootie" Johnson, then the chairman of Augusta National. It was a battle that elicited some colorful and defiant trash talk. It was a battle that led to a demonstration in a muddy field just down Washington Road from Magnolia Lane on the Saturday of the 2003 Masters that turned into an embarrassing sideshow with the KKK and an Elvis impersonator showing up and more reporters present than demonstrators on hand.

But it was a battle that—in either a big way or a little—helped open Magnolia Lane to at least some female members.

———

The Impetus

It all began on April 11, 2002, when Burk read a newspaper article quoting Johnson saying, "We have no exclusionary policies as far as our membership is concerned."

Burk, on behalf of the NCWO, sent a nine-sentence letter to Johnson demanding that he "open [his] membership to women now, so that this is not an issue when the tournament is staged next year."

Johnson's public response turned out to be a wildly ill-advised move that became a public relations fiasco for the club.

"We do not intend to become a trophy in their display case," Johnson ranted in a response letter to Burk. "There may well come a day when women will be invited to join our membership but that timetable will be ours, and not at the point of a bayonet. I have found your letter's several references to discrimination, allusions to sponsors and your setting of deadlines to be both offensive and coercive. Any further communication between us would not be productive."

Johnson's outrage to Burk's letter ignited a national debate and, eventually, the demonstration Burk engineered. It was a demonstration that cost the city of Augusta $120,000 in a settlement after a Circuit Court of Appeals later agreed that Burk's rights had been violated when her group was forced to protest in that muddy field away from the club instead of outside the gates of Augusta National.

Following the Burk–Johnson public bruhaha, two of the Masters' major corporate sponsors—Coca-Cola and IBM—along with its broadcast partner, CBS, and the PGA Tour, issued statements shying away from the topic by saying that it is inappropriate for them to comment on Augusta's membership policies.

"I don't think it's for us to be concerned about," then–PGA Tour commissioner Tim Finchem said. "We don't have a contractual obligation with Augusta National."

The matter took an explosive turn on July 16, 2002, when Tiger Woods, in a pre-tournament press conference at the British Open at Muirfield, was asked about Augusta National's exclusionary policy preventing female members.

"[Augusta National is] entitled to set up their own rules the way they want them," Woods said. "That's the way they want to set it up. It's their prerogative to set it up that way. It would be nice to see everyone have an equal chance to participate if they wanted to, but there is nothing you can do about it…it's just the way it is."

Woods' words were shocking considering that his early existence in golf was all about opening doors to those who were excluded because of prejudice, emphasized by his first Nike TV commercial that blared against his exclusion from certain golf clubs because of the color of his skin.

The immediate fallout was a front-page column in the *New York Post* with a large block-letter headline screaming HYPOCRITE ripping him for being "gutless" with his "straddle-the-fence answer" to the question about women not being allowed as members of Augusta National.

Woods' stature in the game, as not only the best player in the world but probably the most recognized golfer on the planet, was such that he could have made a difference if he wanted to. Yet, intensely protective and careful about his image, this was the greatest example of all on how he constantly refused to take public stands on any issues.

"I find it shocking and appalling that somebody who has brought so much stature to the game of golf is basically saying it's all right to discriminate against humans," Charles Farrell, the director of Rainbow Sports, a division of Jesse Jackson's Rainbow Push Wall Street Project for expanded opportunities for minorities (including women) in the sports industry, told *The Post* in that column.

"When he first turned pro, his whole TV [commercial] campaign was about the places that wouldn't let him play because of race. That was very dramatic and very effective, and there were some clubs that had excluded blacks that opened doors to blacks because of the pressure that came from [Woods'] comments.

"To condone discriminating against women I think plays right into the hands of those who would want things back the way they were before 1954," continued Farrell. "Tiger Woods has brought such enormity to the game of golf that his comments to the negative side of this sets us back 20 to 30 years. It's very disappointing to see a person of color represent that kind of thinking."

Farrell said he was certain that if Woods took a stand and even threatened to pull out of a tournament played at a club where women were excluded, those clubs would open to women members in a hurry.

Woods, a three-time Masters winner at Augusta, was asked at that time if, with his stature in the game, he could force a change.

"I've done my part so far trying to get more kids who haven't been able to have access to the game; that's what my foundation is about," he said.

Farrell countered, "I see a lot of those kids at his [Tiger Woods Foundation] clinics are young girls. What kind of message is he sending to those young girls who are coming up and saying,

'I want to be like Tiger?' To condemn them to a second-class golf citizenship I think is absurd. It's very sad."

Woods, who is of African American and Asian descent, was asked if he felt this discrimination against women also applies to African Americans and Asians.

"Yes, I do," he said.

It seemed alarming that the most influential person in sports had allowed himself to acquiesce to the blatant discrimination and simply pass it off with such an ignorant default statement that amounted to, "It is what it is."

Woods' statement infuriated Burk, who quickly responded.

"Tiger Woods is uniquely positioned to help make changes and should reconsider his notion that nothing can be done," Burk told the *Washington Post*.

"We will not take the view that some have, [that] Tiger has spoken and now it's over," Burk said in an interview with the *New York Times*. "It is not over. For all my respect for him, Tiger is naive when it comes to changing course."

Several weeks later, Woods resorted to damage control with a statement he released on his website, tigerwoods.com. It read: "Would I like to see women members? Yes, that would be great, but I am only one voice. Everyone has to understand that Augusta isn't quick to change. No matter what I or the press says, they do things at their own pace...and won't buckle to outside pressure."

With pressure mounting from Burk's crusade, which included letters to the Masters corporate sponsors, Johnson announced on August 30, 2002, that the tournament was dropping its three sponsors—Citigroup, Coca-Cola, and IBM—and would telecast the 2003 tournament commercial-free. That, according to reports, cost the club an estimated $20 million.

"Augusta National is [the NCWO's] true target," Johnson said at the time. "It is therefore unfair to put the Masters' media sponsors in the position of having to deal with this pressure. It's not their fight."

Burk attempted to push CBS into dropping its coverage of the Masters, an attempt that the network never took seriously.

Sean McManus, the president of CBS Sports, told Burk that not televising the Masters "would be a disservice to fans of this major championship."

In October 2002, Burk announced that she planned to conduct a protest outside the gates of Augusta National during Masters week.

In November, Johnson broke a four-month stretch in which he'd remained silent, meeting individually with representatives from the *New York Times*, the Associated Press, the *Augusta Chronicle* and *Sports Illustrated* at Augusta National to spread his and the club's message. The news organizations were each given an hour to interview Johnson and agreed to embargo their interviews until 9:00 PM on November 11.

ESPN.com broke the embargo by running the AP's Q&A with Johnson in the afternoon, in which he said the club had no intention of admitting a female member by April, that it had no timetable for doing so, and that 99 percent of the membership agreed with him.

In a *Wall Street Journal* op-ed piece, Johnson wrote, "The notion that Augusta National is an enclave of sexist good old boys is ludicrous," and that the club would continue in its "resolve not to be told what to do by an individual who knows nothing about us."

With Masters week approaching, Burk submitted an application for a permit to demonstrate in Augusta in early March of 2002. It was for 200 protesters across the street from the main gate of the club on Masters Saturday.

On the surface, the demonstration was a disaster. It took place a half-mile down Washington Road from the club and it looked more like a series of depressing carnival acts than a serious demonstration.

There was an inflatable pig and an Elvis impersonator. There was a Ku Klux Klan Imperial Wizard named J.J. Harper and a flag-draped drag queen named Georgina Z. Bush.

"Augusta is all about Applebee's and boredom, so we certainly livened up the place," Burk told reporters. "The protest did not net the result that we wanted but beyond that, we accomplished our goal. We kept the issue in the media for a year. We wouldn't be talking about it now if not."

Influence

It's difficult to argue that Burk did not become one of the most influential figures in Augusta National history with her activism in 2002.

Though there is no hard evidence backing this up, it's very likely that Burk's work influenced several significant upgrades the club made for its Masters week experience in an effort to improve its image.

The Par-3 Contest, which annually includes players having their young kids caddie for them, is now televised live. A "Drive, Chip, and Putt Contest" was started for young boys and girls. And, in 2019, the Augusta National Women's Amateur was born. Both events take place in the two days before the Masters begins.

The most tangible evidence of Burk's influence on Augusta National came in 2012, when the club announced that Condoleeza Rice, a former Secretary of State, and Darla Moore, a South Carolina financier, were invited in as its first two female members.

"This is a joyous occasion," Augusta National chairman Billy Payne told the Associated Press the day the two women became members.

"Oh my God, we won," Burk told the AP.

Even Johnson, who had since retired as chairman in 2006 and died in 2017, said of the news in a statement to *The State* newspaper in Columbia, South Carolina, "This is wonderful news for Augusta National Golf Club and I could not be more pleased. Darla Moore is my good friend, and I know she and Condoleezza Rice will enjoy the Club as much as I have."

Payne, who took over for Johnson as chairman in 2006 (and was replaced by Fred Ridley in 2017), said consideration for new members was deliberate and private and that Rice and Moore were not treated differently from other new members. Still, though, he took the rare step of announcing two of the latest members to join because of the historical significance.

"These accomplished women share our passion for the game of golf and both are well known and respected by our membership," Payne said in a statement. "It will be a proud moment when we present Condoleezza and Darla their green jackets when the club opens this fall. This is a significant and positive time in our club's history and, on behalf of our membership, I wanted to take this opportunity to welcome them and all of our new members into the Augusta National family."

Significant figures in the game quickly began to weigh in.

Woods, who knew Rice through a connection at Stanford University, where he went to school, said in a statement, "I think the decision by the Augusta National membership is important to golf. The Club continues to demonstrate its commitment to impacting the game in positive ways. I would like to congratulate both new members, especially my friend Condi Rice."

Upon the news of Rice being admitted into Augusta, Woods also had a snide message for me, since I was the reporter who'd written that *New York Post* column calling him out as a hypocrite after that press conference at the 2002 British Open. Woods and his handlers were livid at the column, and Woods never forgot.

During a practice round for the PGA Tour's FedEx Cup Playoff event at Bethpage Black in 2012, Woods quietly made a beeline to me from the fairway as I followed his practice round and said sarcastically, "Well, you must be happy about Condi Rice getting into Augusta."

Ten years later, Woods had not forgotten that column I wrote and couldn't help himself from taking a dig at me.

Jack Nicklaus, who owns the record for most Masters victories with six and is an Augusta member, said, "Everyone at Augusta National shares a similar passion for the game of golf, and I know they will be great additions to the club."

Tim Finchem, the PGA Tour commissioner at the time, said, "At a time when women represent one of the fastest growing segments in both playing and following the game of golf, this sends a positive and inclusive message for our sport."

The Associated Press quoted sources who said that Rice and Moore first were considered as members in 2007, which would have been four years after the 2003 Masters, when Burk's protest took place, and one year after Payne took over as chairman.

"It came sooner than I expected," Burk told the AP. "I thought they were going to try to outlast me, and I really thought they would wait until the women's movement would get no credit. But if we had not done what we did, this would not have happened now."

Rice was the national security advisor under former president George W. Bush and became secretary of state in his second term. She was the first black woman to be a Stanford provost in 1993.

Since her admittance to Augusta, she has been very visible during Masters week wearing her green jacket. She's become good friends with the likes of Phil Mickelson, who plays golf with her on occasion and annually has lunch with her and some other members during Masters week on the veranda of the clubhouse.

"I have visited Augusta National on several occasions and look forward to playing golf, renewing friendships, and forming new ones through this very special opportunity," Rice said in a statement released by the club upon her admittance. "I have long admired the important role Augusta National has played in the traditions and history of golf. I also have an immense respect for the Masters Tournament and its commitment to grow the game of golf, particularly with youth, here in the United States and throughout the world."

Moore in the 1980s with Chemical Bank became the highest-paid woman in the banking industry. She was the first woman to be profiled on the cover of *Fortune* magazine, and in 1998 she made an initial $25 million contribution to her alma mater, the University of South Carolina, which renamed its business school after her. She later gave the school an additional $45 million in 2004.

"Augusta National has always captured my imagination, and is one of the most magically beautiful places anywhere in the world, as everyone gets to see during the Masters each April," Moore said in a statement upon her admittance. "I am fortunate to have many friends who are members at Augusta National, so to be asked to join them as a member represents a very happy and important occasion in my life. Above all, Augusta National and the Masters tournaments have always stood for excellence, and that is what is so important to me."

This all seemed a long way from Hootie Johnson's words to the Associated Press in 2002 when he defiantly said, "Our club has enjoyed a camaraderie and a closeness that's served us well for so long, that it makes it difficult for us to consider change. A woman may be a member of this club one day, but that is out in the future."

While proud of whatever difference she made, Burk, over the years, has not sounded completely satisfied with the change at Augusta National, actually remaining rather cynical.

In a 2013 article by Burk in the *Huffington Post*, she wrote: "Condoleezza Rice looks like she's having a great time—and more power to her. Someone emailed me to ask if I didn't think she maybe owes me a beer. Sure she does—me and a lot of others standing in that muddy field a decade ago. If we hadn't been there then, women wouldn't have the right to network with their big-business peers and play those manicured greens now."

This was a passage from what Burk wrote in another *Huffington Post* article ahead of the 2015 Masters: "The Green Dinos at Augusta National Golf Club will wine, dine, and brag about how their club is so exclusive the membership roster is secret. Well, mostly secret. If someone shows up at the tourney sporting a new green jacket, that means they've been allowed into the hoariest of old boys clubs.

"Augusta finally opened the gates a crack in 2012 and let two women squeeze through. It was hardly a breakthrough. The club famously snubbed Virginia Rometty, the new CEO of main tournament sponsor IBM, even though the male CEOs before her at Big Blue had been promptly welcomed into the fold. Last November, the boys relented and let Rometty in. In 25 years, will there still be only three token women?"

In a 2015 interview with *Sports Illustrated*, Burk said, "I definitely lit the fuse in changing Augusta National. They would be closed to women right now if we hadn't done what we did."

PART SEVEN

SUNDAY

Chapter 21

THE SHARK

Golf can be a cruel game. Augusta National sometimes can make it even crueler. Ask Greg Norman.

The pioneering Australian, who became known as the "Great White Shark" for his dominating prowess on the golf course and off it as an entrepreneur, was reduced to a minnow at Augusta National.

Twenty-three times Norman played in the Masters and 23 times he walked away disappointed, and sometimes devastated. No player in the Masters history has had more gut-wrenching close calls without reward than Norman. No player in the history of the game has been more associated with epic failure at a single major tournament than Norman at the Masters.

Norman was the bridesmaid to Jack Nicklaus' remarkable sixth career green jacket victory in 1986 at age 46. He was tied with Nicklaus after carding a birdie on the 17th hole. He hit his tee shot on the par-4 18th into the fairway, but pushed his approach shot into the gallery and bogeyed the hole, leaving Nicklaus to win by one stroke.

He stood helplessly on the 11th hole and watched Larry Mize, a likeable Augusta native, chip in from 45 yards for birdie and a playoff walk-off victory in 1987, Mize's only career major championship win.

None of Norman's close calls, though, were more painful than 1996, when he let a six-shot lead leak agonizingly away in the final round to lose to Nick Faldo.

Even if you were not rooting for Norman, that one was painful to watch for everyone who witnessed it, even Faldo, who copped his third green jacket at Norman's expense. On the way off the 18th green on the Sunday, Faldo, who'd shot 67 to Norman's staggering 78, consoled Norman as if his foe had just lost a family member.

Faldo, known for his aloof, stoic demeanor, had tears in his eyes as he and Norman walked off the 18th green, his arm around Norman. And those tears surely were as much for the man whose will he'd crushed as for his own accomplishment.

"I feel for him," Faldo said afterward. "What he's been through is horrible. It's hard to be plastered and repair that. He's had a real rough ride. I hope I'll be remembered for shooting a 67 on the last day and storming through. But obviously, it'll be remembered for what happened to Greg."

Norman, who was vying to become the first Australian to win a Masters (Adam Scott later would become the first, in 2013), owns the dubious distinction as the only player to lose all four major championships in a playoff.

As a closer, he was no Mariano Rivera. He won only one of the seven majors he led entering the final round. Nicklaus, by comparison, won 10 of the 12 majors he led after 54 holes.

"I played like shit," Norman said. "That's the best way to say it. I wouldn't like to see a player do what I did. Nobody would. I screwed up. I put all the blame on myself. People can write and say whatever they wish, but it wasn't nerves or impatience.

My rhythm went haywire. That happens in golf. But this mess-up came at the worst of times.

"I didn't choke, although critics will say I did. I just played rotten while Nick was playing great golf. I just screwed up. I never felt tight. Never felt tension in the body or the mind. No tension in my game."

As memorable as what happened on the golf course that day was the way Norman conducted himself afterward. He was classy, accountable, dignified, and even a touch defiant.

"I just didn't win today," Norman would say afterward. "I'm not a loser. I am a winner. I'm not a loser. I'm not a loser in life. I just lost a golf tournament. Maybe there is a reason for what I have inflicted on myself. Maybe something good will happen to me. All this is just a test."

Norman still had a five-shot lead through the fifth hole, but there was a sense that he wasn't right. Faldo birdied the sixth and eighth holes and those, combined with Norman bogeys at the ninth, 10th, and 11th, put them in a tie.

Norman's wedge approach shot spun back off the green on the ninth, leading to bogey. At the 10th, a poor chip led to another bogey. And at 11, Norman thought he'd made his birdie putt, but saw it slide by and he then missed the comebacker for par, taking another bogey.

"It was evident he was ruined through the middle of the round," Faldo said. "That's what really opened the doors up. I just had to play my game and keep the pressure on."

Norman insisted, "I never felt tight. The only thing I felt was I lost my rhythm. I lost my timing a little bit. I didn't feel any tension. I just played poorly."

Fittingly, it was at Amen Corner where it effectively ended for Norman, who hit his tee shot into the water at the par-3 12th

and took double bogey, leaving him two shots behind Faldo. He never would recover.

"I felt it slipping away at No. 12," Norman said. "I knew it was gone at No. 16 (where he also hit his tee shot into the water). I let it get away. I'm very disappointed. Of all of them I let get away, this one I did let get away. Even if I had played halfway decent, it would have been a good tussle with Nick. I let it slip. I made a lot of mistakes. I just didn't get the job done."

No player had squandered a larger 54-hole lead in a major championship since 1910. Perhaps it was fitting that this Norman sunk ship came on the 84th anniversary of the sinking of the Titanic. Honest.

Mickelson, who finished third, said, "My heart goes out to him because he's an excellent player and a true champion and it just wasn't his day. I don't know what the deal was. He played excellent golf the first three rounds. It's hard for me to imagine that 78."

Nick Price, a close friend of Norman's, was finished with his round and in the clubhouse watching on a television and he finally had to look away, saying, "I can't even watch."

"If this were my last Masters, I'd be disappointed that I'd never won," Norman said. "It's the greatest championship in the world. God, I'd love to put on a green jacket, but it's not the end. I'm going to play here again, and I'm not going to fall off the end of the Earth.

"I'm very, very philosophical about things. That's one of my strong points, that I can approach life in that regard. Hey, of course I screwed this one up bad. It's definitely the most disappointing round of my career. But not everything's perfect your whole life. Maybe these hiccups that I've inflicted on myself are meant for another reason. I mean, that's how I think. I think there's something good waiting for me down the line."

As level-headed as Norman was, his fellow players were devastated for him, perhaps putting themselves in his shoes and shuddering at the mere thought of such anguish.

"This is tough for him; you have to feel terrible to lose a lead like that," Duffy Waldorf, who finished tied for fifth, said. "I felt he was uncatchable. I figured he could have shot even-par and still won. I don't think anybody else really thought they had a realistic chance to catch him."

Scott McCarron said, "It's kind of hard to feel sorry for Greg because of all that he's done, but you had to today because he had it in the bag. I guess those things happen at the Masters. But Greg's the best player in the world, and he's still the best. He's going to win this tournament someday."

Someday, of course, would never come for Norman at Augusta.

"I will awaken Monday morning, I trust, and will get down to Hilton Head to go on with PGA Tour work," Norman said. "My life is pretty good. It's not the end of my world, losing this Masters."

———

The Big Lead

A 1-under-par 71 in the third round on Saturday had Norman in the driver's seat, sitting comfortably with a six-shot lead at a tournament where no player had ever blown a six-shot lead in its 59 previous editions.

It was, however, the seventh time that Norman had entered the final round of a major with a lead, and he'd won only one of those, the 1986 British Open.

"I don't live in the past," Norman said on that Saturday. "I don't dwell on those things. I feel comfortable."

Norman's 54-hole total of 203 had him standing at 13 under par, with the Masters scoring record of 17 under (set by Jack Nicklaus in 1965 and tied by Ray Floyd in 1976) within reach.

"I'll try to come to the first tee feeling as comfortable and relaxed as I have the first three days," he said. "I'll treat it as if nobody is in the lead, pretend we all have the same score. I feel pretty good, but I've still got a lot of work to do. There's no sense getting excited now. I'm going to enjoy tomorrow no matter what happens. I'll try to enjoy it every step of the way.

"Irrespective of what happens, I'm going to enjoy every step I take. I've got a chance to win the Masters. I've been there before. There's no better feeling than having a chance to win a major championship."

Faldo, who was six shots back after Saturday, said, "I'm a long way back, but anything's possible. It's all gain and nothing to lose. Just go out and play."

Through three rounds, Norman had only one bogey on the back nine and 11 birdies. He'd birdied two par-5s on the back, No. 13 and No. 15, in all three rounds.

Asked on Saturday if anyone could catch Norman, Phil Mickelson said, "Well, I don't know. What do you think? I think that anything's possible, so I don't want to rule out the improbable."

Those turned out to be prophetic words from Mickelson.

A Letter

In the aftermath of Norman's Masters collapse, Scott Hoch sent a letter to Norman. The crux of the message: Been there. Done that.

"I felt terrible for him," Hoch told the Associated Press. "I was one person who could definitely commiserate with him."

Seven years earlier, Hoch was standing over a two-and-a-half-foot putt to win the Masters in a playoff with Nick Faldo. Hoch missed the putt and Faldo went on to win the first of his three green jackets on the next hole.

While Norman, perhaps because of all the major championship calamity he'd endured, was a sympathetic figure in the wake of that Masters loss, the media wasn't so sympathetic toward Hoch.

"They stabbed me pretty good," Hoch said.

When Hoch lost his close-call Masters, he joked to reporters that if he had a gun, he might have shot himself. A columnist followed that up by writing that it was a good thing he didn't because, with his aim, someone in the gallery could have been hurt.

"They [the media] weren't sympathetic toward me like they were toward Greg," Hoch recalled. "I thought they were kind of easy on [Norman]. He received what he should have, but they were pretty rough on me. All I did was miss a two-foot putt after playing awfully well the rest of the day. He played poorly all day."

Hoch won six times on the PGA Tour and won millions of dollars, but he never won a major championship, which makes that missed Masters opportunity one that he'll never forget.

"I don't know if you ever get over it," he said.

Norman, ever the optimist, tried.

When he returned to Augusta a year later, Norman revealed that he'd spent some time before that 1997 Masters with motivational speaker Tony Robbins, he of late-night infomercial fame.

Robbins visited Norman's house days before that Masters carrying an 800-page dossier on Norman.

"Tony's very motivational," Norman said at the time. "He doesn't want to get into your head and tell you how to play the game. He's never played the game. He doesn't know anything about the game. But he understands how to motivate people. What I got out of it was just reminding myself of who I am and how good I am, because you forget about all that. I was re-educating myself. That's all I was doing."

Part of the Robbins therapy was getting Norman to purge the bad times from his mind and focus on the good things he'd done—like the rounds in the low-to-mid 60s he'd shot at Augusta and not the 78 he threw down in the final round in '96.

"If you keep thinking about the worst round you've ever had in your life, you're going to keep playing that same crappy round," Norman said. "Flush it out. I don't want to keep thinking about it."

Norman later conceded that in the immediate aftermath of the loss, his collapse did adversely affect him.

"I was very angry with myself that day," Norman said of the final round. "Monday I was fine. Tuesday I was very angry with myself just for the emotion of everything. By the time I got back in the office and got home, it was gone. I am a very resilient guy. It's going to take a bigger bullet than that to stop me."

He recounted his annual spring vacation going deep-sea fishing in Mexico on his 87-foot yacht, Aussie Rules. He said the only round of golf he played was for fun, saying, "I drank 18 bottles of beer on 18 holes and had a great time."

Norman, who said he got more than 7,500 letters of encouragement from people, said the loss "changed my life."

"Each and every one of them had a meaning," Norman said. "It makes me feel better to be a father. My kids look up to me now. I am not as cynical now. I feel totally different about my whole approach to life and the world. I know I am a better person for it. I know I'm not a loser, as I said after the Masters. I know I have a lot of golf left in me. People have their perceptions.

They want to call you a choker or gagger. But in reality, they are not the ones there.

"The bad thing is that I didn't win," Norman went on. "The good thing is that it changed my life. I've never felt anything as powerful. It was a huge emotional lift, an overwhelming experience. I feel like I'm a different person now. A better person. Sometimes you get better things from not winning. This has definitely made me feel better. It was probably the tonic I need to carry on until I retire."

Chapter 22

SPIETH

Augusta National makes some players, and it breaks others. Jordan Spieth is one of those rare players who's experienced both extremes, and they came a year apart. Spieth won the Masters in 2015, and he should have won it in 2016, but he choked. That's right: he choked.

There's no shame in that. More accomplished players than Spieth, who's one of the great young players of the current generation, have thrown away major championships as their throats tightened in the cauldron of intense pressure and expectation.

One year after Spieth captured the 2015 Masters, he stood on the 10th tee in the final round with a five-shot lead.

And did not win.

—————

Nine Holes Remaining

The tournament was over.

The final result of the 80th Masters was a foregone conclusion.

The only chore that seemingly remained for Spieth, who looked like he owned the tournament from his opening tee shot Thursday, was a trip to Butler Cabin, where he would slip the green jacket over his own shoulders as the defending champion.

Then all hell broke loose around Amen Corner.

Spieth, 22 at the time, was poised to win his second consecutive Masters and take over the No. 1 world ranking.

And then he did neither.

When the violent tornado had finally passed through Augusta National on an unforgettable Sunday afternoon, it had turned the tournament upside down and left Englishman Danny Willett, who, playing ahead of Spieth, quietly carded a final-round 67, as the winner at 5-under par and Spieth a stunning distant runner-up at 2-under.

Everything changed for everyone involved on No. 12—the centerpiece of Amen Corner and arguably the most famous par-3 in golf. In a shocking turn of events, Spieth authored one of the greatest collapses in not only Masters history but in major championship history when he took a quadruple bogey 7 on No. 12.

The carnage began with Spieth hitting his tee shot into Rae's Creek.

"It's a stock 9-iron for me," Spieth said. "I didn't take that extra deep breath and really focus on my line on 12. Instead, I went up and I just put a quick swing on it. It was a lack of discipline to hit it over the bunker coming off two bogeys, instead of recognizing I was still leading the Masters.

"Boy, you wonder about not only just the tee shot on 12, but why can't you just control the second shot, you know, and make 5 at the worst, and you're still tied for the lead?"

Incredibly, Spieth recalled making a similar mistake at No. 12 in 2014, when he took bogey and ended up finishing second.

"I remember getting over the ball thinking I'm going to go ahead and hit a little cut to the hole, and that's what I did in 2014 and it cost me the tournament then, too," he said. "That was the right club, just the wrong shot. I was more comfortable hitting a draw with my iron. I knew every time I played a fade this week, that shot kind of came out. At the time, you're going to throw all bad swings away and you're just going to focus on how confident you can step into that shot and that's what I did. But the swing just wasn't quite there to produce the right ball flight. So ultimately I should have just played a draw on that hole."

After the first ball in the creek, Spieth took a penalty drop in the shallow portion of the 13th fairway and chunked his next shot into the middle of the water—a shot you'd expect to see from a nervous 20 handicapper afraid to hit over a water hazard.

His fifth shot landed in the back bunker and, after he splashed out and made the putt, Spieth had scored a 7 on the hole—the highest score he'd ever posted in a major championship.

To put it in further perspective, Spieth had needed only eight strokes to play the par-3 12th hole during his first three rounds and seven shots on Sunday to complete it. As agonizing as it was for Spieth to experience, it was agony to watch—for everyone, whether they were witnessing it in person or from the safety of their couch on television.

"It just kind of stunk to watch it," said Smylie Kaufman, who was paired with Spieth in the final round.

"I can't imagine that was fun for everyone to experience—other than Danny's team and those who are fans of him," Spieth would say later.

"I think the whole golfing world feels for Jordan Spieth," Jack Nicklaus posted on his Twitter account. "He had a chance to do something truly special and something very few have done before—and be the youngest to accomplish that—and he just didn't pull through. My heart goes out to him for what happened, but I know that Jordan is a young man who will certainly learn from this experience and there will be some good that comes out of this for him. He's a wonderful talent and a wonderful young man."

Spieth carried a five-shot lead as he made the turn thanks to consecutive birdies on Nos. 6, 7, 8, and 9, and he looked in complete command. "It was a dream-come-true front nine," he said.

But he began to show signs of nerves with bogeys on No. 10 and No. 11. And then 12 happened.

"Just a lapse of concentration on 12 and it cost me," he said.

It cost him a chance at history, a chance to become only the fourth player ever to defend his Masters title.

Spieth, who finished second in his first Masters in 2014, and won it in 2015, entered the day having owned the lead in his previous seven rounds at Augusta, a Masters record. None of that mattered by about 7:15 PM, when Spieth staggered off the 18th green looking like he'd just gone 10 rounds with Mike Tyson in his prime—three shots behind Willett, the accidental-tourist winner.

"It's all rather surreal right now," Willett said.

Spieth was gutted afterward.

He had converted his previous five 54-hole leads into victories—two of those major championships.

"It was just a very tough 30 minutes for me that hopefully I never experience again," he said.

As he stood on the 12th tee, Spieth was 5-under par and had a one-shot lead over Willett. When he walked off the 12th green, he was 1-under par trailing Willett by three shots. He made a couple of game comeback birdies on Nos. 13 and 15, but never fully recovered.

"It all happened very, very quick," Willett said.

Jason Day said he was on the 15th hole when he looked at the scoreboard and saw the carnage. "I was absolutely shocked when I saw Jordan go from 5 to 1," Day said.

"Anything can happen at Augusta—especially at Amen Corner," said Lee Westwood, who tied for second with Spieth at 2-under. "It's a fine line between disaster and success at this place, and it happened to Jordan. Championship golf can throw in some shocks sometimes."

As if what he'd endured during the final 90 minutes of the tournament was not painful enough, taking part in the traditional green jacket ceremony at Butler Cabin and then on the 18th green must have felt like it took 90 days to Spieth.

"I can't think of anybody else who may have had a tougher ceremony to experience," Spieth said.

In a quiet moment during the green jacket ceremony, Willett, the son of a vicar in England, told Spieth that "maybe fate" had decided this was his time.

"I certainly wanted to control fate myself," Spieth said.

The Masters so often shows even the best in the game that they cannot control their own fate.

"Big picture, this one will hurt," Spieth said. "It will take a while."

Fortunately, for him, it would not take long, as he would exorcise any final-round major-championship demons he had with a win at the British Open in 2017.

———

In Position to Win

It sometimes is difficult to breathe when you're in rarefied air.

This was the challenge Spieth faced while trying to defend his Masters title in that final round. The way he performed in 2015—winning five times, including two major championships—Spieth raised the bar so high you wondered whether he would need an oxygen mask to breathe.

His ascent to the top of the golf world gave him a glimpse into the world where Tiger Woods once resided. It is a world of unrealistic expectations that can sometimes suffocate those who are expected to succeed every time they show up. It is a world created by special athletes whose performances are so dominant they can become victims of their own success.

Woods lived in this world for a decade and a half and he thrived in it. Spieth was a visitor to that world and found it rather hot inside.

Spieth was attempting to become only the fourth player to defend his Masters title. He, too, was trying to win his fourth major championship at the age of 22. This is how Spieth's career Masters record would have looked if he were able to close that 2016 Masters out: runner-up, win, win. Had Spieth sealed the deal, he would have gone wire-to-wire to win the Masters for the second consecutive year. Preposterous stuff.

But Sunday would not come without its challenges. His late free-fall in the third round brought a few players back into contention for the final 18 holes. He had been cruising with a four-shot lead when he stepped to the 17th tee and pushed his drive into the right trees and took bogey. Then, on 18, he hit his tee shot even further right into trees and made a sloppy double bogey.

Suddenly, his four-shot lead was melted to one over Kaufman, two over the remarkable 58-year-old German grinder Bernhard Langer and Japan's Hideki Matsuyama, both of whom were 1-under. World No. 1 Jason Day, Dustin Johnson, and Willett, all deemed afterthoughts before Spieth's late hiccups, were just three shots back at even-par.

"I've got to throw this away, pretend [Sunday] is a new round and everyone is tied and understand that this is the position I wanted to be in after 54 holes and not think about the end to [Saturday's] round," Spieth said after his Saturday round. "It was a really tough finish to go from really holding a four-shot lead and being in a very similar position to last year to where all of the sudden now it's anyone's game. It's tough to swallow that.

"I'm in the lead after 54 holes. If you told me that at the beginning of the week, I'd be obviously very pleased."

The year before, Spieth took a commanding four-shot lead into the final round and cruised to victory. The vibe entering Sunday would be quite a bit different. "I certainly felt better last year on Saturday night than I do right now," Spieth said.

"He's been in control of this golf tournament from the first day," said Rory McIlroy, who was paired with Spieth in the third round. "I haven't got a green jacket. He has. So, there's added pressure that comes with that, too. So, we'll see what happens. He's sitting on top of the leaderboard...so it's his to lose."

So it was.

And it all came unglued on the 12th hole, a hole that Jack Nicklaus once called "the most dangerous par-3 in the game."

The 12th hole at Augusta has altered many lives in the past. Tom Weiskopf posted the highest score in Masters history at the hole when he took a 13 on it in 1980. The great Arnold Palmer hit into Rae's Creek in 1959 and it cost him a chance at a second consecutive victory.

The most notorious implosion on No. 12 came from Norman in 1996, when he took double bogey en route to losing a six-shot final-round lead to winner Nick Faldo.

So, Spieth was not alone.

As Spieth walked to his courtesy car in the players parking lot following the devastating loss, Faldo—of all people, the beneficiary of gifts from Norman and Hoch helping him win Masters green jackets—stopped him to offer words of encouragement and shake his hand.

"Greg was right from the word go on a downward trend, and Jordan was on an upward trend," Faldo told reporters that night.

Indeed, Norman already was well into his collapse by the time he and Faldo got to the 12th hole. For Spieth, the quadruple on 12 was so sudden.

Making what happened on the back nine, particularly No. 12, so shocking was that Spieth had closed out the front nine with four consecutive birdies to seemingly put the tournament to sleep.

Then came bogeys on Nos. 10 and 11, which could have been viewed as mere hiccups...until 12 happened.

"At 10 and 11, you can take bogeys there," Spieth said. "I was still 2-under for the tournament with a couple of par-5s left. My goal for the day was 4-under. So we were still right on pace. I just didn't take that extra deep breath."

The first shot in the water didn't cost Spieth. Like in the case with Phil Mickelson en route to blowing the 2006 U.S. Open at Winged Foot, where he famously hit his tee shot on the final hole off a hospitality tent, it was the second shot that doomed Spieth.

Like Mickelson's ill-advised 3-iron that he greedily tried (unsuccessfully) to bend around the trees and up toward the green, it was Spieth's chunked wedge after his drop that killed him. "I'm not really sure what happened on the next shot," Spieth said.

On his walk from the 12th green to the 13th tee, his lead turned into a deficit, Spieth said to his caddie, Michael Greller, "Buddy, it seems like we're collapsing."

Spieth was correct about that except for the tense of his sentence. He should have used the word *collapsed*, because by then it was over.

"This is going to hurt badly," Faldo said. "He was on the steps of doing something to join our little club, which would've been great. I would've welcomed him to our little club of those who have defended. The good news is he's 22. You regroup. He's way too talented. He's got a lot of majors he's going to have a shot to win."

―――――

Famous Masters Meltdowns

1996: Greg Norman lost a six-shot lead, the largest blown 54-hole lead in tournament history, as Nick Faldo shot a final-round 67 to win his third green jacket.

2011: Rory McIlroy began the final round with a four-shot lead and shot 80 to finish tied for 15th. McIlroy came unglued on the back nine, beginning with the 10th hole, where he yanked his tee shot so deep into the woods to the left of the fairway it was near the cabins.

1956: Ken Venturi failed to hold onto a four-shot lead in the final round, shooting 80, and lost to Jack Burke Jr.

1979: Ed Sneed began the final round with a five-shot lead and still led by three with three holes to play, but he bogeyed 16, 17, and 18 and Fuzzy Zoeller won in a playoff in his first Masters.

1986: Seve Ballesteros, rattled by Jack Nicklaus' famous back-nine charge, hit his approach shot to 15 in the water, opening the door for Nicklaus to win his 18th and final major.

1961: Arnold Palmer, needing only a par on the 18th hole to win back-to-back Masters, double-bogeyed the 72nd hole, allowing Gary Player to become the first international champion.

1989: Scott Hoch missed a short par putt on the 17th hole and then, on the first hole of a sudden-death playoff, he missed a two-foot putt that would have given him his first major championship win. Faldo took advantage and made a long birdie putt on the next hole to win his first green jacket.

1980: Curtis Strange had a three-shot lead with six holes to play in the final round and hit into the water on Nos. 13 and 15, finishing two shots behind winner Bernhard Langer.

2009: Kenny Perry had a two-shot lead with two holes to play and he left a putt short on the 72nd hole and lost in a playoff to Ángel Cabrera.

————

Aftermath

About a month after his Masters nightmare, Spieth related a funny story about the public reaction he'd gotten from people when they meet him.

"I've got ladies at the grocery stores putting their hand on me and going, 'Really praying for you. How are you doing?'" Spieth said. "I'm like, 'My dog didn't die. I'll be okay. I'll survive. It happens.'"

When Spieth returned to Augusta for the first time after the 2016 loss, in December 2016, he played with some friends and twice birdied the 12th hole, named Golden Bell.

"The first time back, I was very nervous when I got on the 12th tee," Spieth conceded. "I was playing with friends and I was vocally expressing that, 'Guys, we have some demons to get rid of here, I'd appreciate if y'all stood to the side of the tee box while I do my work here.'

"I hit an 8-iron over the bunker to about 15 feet and my putt fell in for 2. I probably gave like a big fist pump. I was walking around with my hands up, like, 'Demon's gone!' We played it the next morning and I hit a 9-iron this time to a left pin, and it landed about three feet beyond the hole and almost went in. So the last two times I played the hole, I made birdie."

Spieth has not won the Masters since his 2015 triumph, but the demons from 2016 are seemingly gone. Still a young man, he'll undoubtedly have many more chances to win another green jacket.

Chapter 23

RORY

Rory McIlroy has it all.

He's a multi-millionaire 10 times over.

He's happily married.

He has a strong family support system, with parents who've always been by his side and gone out of their way to enhance his chances to become a professional golfer.

He has multiple homes.

He has four career major championships.

He has it all.

Everything except a Masters green jacket.

Among McIlroy's four career major championships are the 2011 U.S. Open, the 2014 British Open, and the 2012 and 2014 PGA Championships. But no Masters, the only victory that separates him from becoming only the sixth player in the history of the game to complete a career Grand Slam by winning each of the four major championships. Only Gene Sarazen, Ben Hogan, Jack Nicklaus, Gary Player, and Tiger Woods have done it.

The lack of a Masters victory is probably the most confounding thing about the too-good-to-be-true twentysomething from

Northern Ireland, because McIlroy should have won at least one Masters—the 2011 iteration, to be precise—but probably a couple more as well.

The question, which still has years remaining before it can be answered based on McIlroy's youth and talent, is whether he becomes one of those bits of Masters history remembered for all the wrong things. A more modern-day Greg Norman, for example. Norman, of course, probably owns the record for most close calls at Augusta National without a trip to the Butler Cabin post-tournament for his own green jacket fitting.

McIlroy, at age 21 and precocious as ever, let the 2011 Masters slip through his hands. At that moment, it felt like a failure to meet great expectations from a golfing prodigy in one of the biggest collapses a major championship had ever seen.

McIlroy carried a four-shot lead into the final round after going 12-under-par for 54 holes but soared to a stunning, tear-filled 80 that left him 10 shots behind South African winner Charl Schwartzel.

"I'm very disappointed at the minute, and I'm sure I will be for the next few days," the classy, curly-haired McIlroy told reporters after the carnage was complete. "But I'll get over it."

Not since Norman squandered a six-stroke lead going into the final round of the 1996 Masters to finish five shots behind champion Nick Faldo had there been such a stunning final-day reversal at Augusta National.

McIlroy showed some early nerves, missing three putts of six feet and closer, but still clung to a one-shot advantage heading into the homeward half. That, however, is when things began to get ugly.

McIlroy hit a monstrously wild drive at the 10th on his way to a triple-bogey, 3-putted for bogey at 11 and 4-putted for double-bogey at the par-3 12th.

"I just hit a poor tee shot on 10 and I just sort of unraveled from there, just sort of lost it on 10, 11, 12, and couldn't really get it back," McIlroy would say later. "It's one of those things. I've got to take the positives, and the positives were that I led this tournament for 63 holes."

The 10th hole was the most famous and most photographed of the day's slide. McIlroy pulled his tee shot into the woods to the left where a pinball-like ricochet off trees sent his ball between two of the Augusta National residential cabins that are dotted around the course and rarely seen during the championship—by fans or television cameras.

In the television shots and still photographs of McIlroy back near those cabins, miles off the 10th fairway, he looked like a boy lost in the woods, unable to process where he was or what was happening to him—even with his caddie, J.P. Fitzgerald, by his side doing everything he could to settle his player down.

After hooking his drive into the pines, McIlroy tried to hit a fairway metal on his next shot and it went wildly left once again. An attempted punch-out to the fairway on the next shot caught the limb of an overhanging tree.

When it was all over, McIlroy took a triple-bogey 7 that dropped him from first place to a tie for seventh, and it was all over. After not taking a single 3-putt in the event, McIlroy used seven putts on the next two holes to seal his fate. After hitting 9-iron onto the green on No. 12, he 4-putted.

"I can't really put my finger on it," he said. "I lost a lot of confidence in my putting around the turn. I didn't really get anything going and was sort of second-guessing lines and second-guessing my speed. On these greens you can't do that."

By the time he got to the par-5 13th hole, his round—and championship hopes—already long run off the rails, McIlroy had tears in his eyes after he hit a ball into Rae's Creek.

It was all such a shift from the McIlroy we'd been talking to during the week, the McIlroy who was laughing about the soccer and football games he and his best mates, Ricky McCormick and Mitchell Tweedie, were playing after the golf at the home they were renting near the golf course. It was an utterly carefree McIlroy, seemingly about to win the Masters at age 21.

And then he was en route to throwing away seven strokes in 12 holes. And he seemed so alone doing it.

With McIlroy having his boyhood friends with him that week, his parents, who usually traveled with him to big tournaments, stayed home and watched it on TV.

"Rosie and I didn't go because he was taking his mates that week," Gerry recalled. "Now I sometimes say to myself, 'Maybe I should have been there.' But that's hindsight."

Tweedie recalled the agony of watching from outside the ropes.

"It was tough for us to watch," he said. "As it was going on, we kind of understood what was going on. He dealt with it very well. That's just him. I'd probably have my putter wrapped around someone's head."

Stephen Crooks, the Holywood head professional at the time, watched from home as McIlroy unraveled with a triple-bogey on the 10th hole, a 4-putt double on 12, and a drive into the creek on 13.

"On the 13th tee, I wanted to be there and give him a hug," Crooks said. "I just really felt sorry for him, because he knew at that stage it was over. Americans, who I know loved him to that point, but after what happened to him and the way he handled himself everyone just fell in love with him."

Paul Gray, the Holywood Golf Club general manager, called the way McIlroy handled himself at Augusta "very brave."

"Between walking off that 18th green and signing his score-card, I think he made the decision subconsciously that this was the starting point for getting over this and putting it behind him and moving on," Gray said. "It's not who he was."

McIlroy, at such a young age, showed his maturity by trying to put the painful experience in perspective afterward with this reasoning: "I'll have plenty more chances. I know that."

At that moment, it felt like McIlroy was trying to talk himself into that possibility as much as he was trying to talk everyone else around him into it. But he had finished in third place in three of the previous five majors and had looked to be heading for a Masters victory. So there certainly was reason to be optimistic—about that Masters and many more to come afterward.

Among the many lessons learned for McIlroy there was one that resonated most: when he took that four-shot lead into the final round, McIlroy changed his demeanor. And the move backfired.

"I came out and was trying to be this player that I'm not," McIlroy said. "I was trying to be ultra-focused, tunnel-visioned, which just isn't like me. I'm usually pretty chatty and sort of looking around and being quite relaxed about the whole thing. However you've played those first three days, try not to change anything. You just have to try to be the same person."

McIlroy called his worst career day on a golf course "very disappointing," but added, "Hopefully, it'll build a little bit of character in me, as well."

Runner-up Adam Scott of Australia called McIlroy "a hell of a player," adding, "He just needs to let it get out of his system and reset everything and get on with it."

Schwartzel, the winner that week, said, "Golf is a really funny game. One moment you're on top of it and the next it bites you. He's such a phenomenal player. He'll win one."

Will he?

McIlroy would tie for 40th in 2012, the year after the debacle. Then there was a tie for 25th in 2013. He finished tied for eighth in 2014, was solo fourth in 2015, then a tie for 10th, seventh, and fifth followed in 2016, '17, and '18 before a tie for 21st in 2019. He finished tied for fifth in 2020, his third career top-five finish at Augusta.

Of course, there's plenty of time for McIlroy to win a Masters and complete the career Grand Slam, but will there always be baggage for him when he drives down Magnolia Lane?

———

Early Years

McIlroy was a mere 2 years old when he first hit a golf shot some 40 yards with a plastic club that his dad Gerry had bought for him.

By the time he was four, he was chipping balls along the halls of his house, which was located across the street from the local golf club, Holywood, and into his mom, Rosie's, washing machine. Gerry had built a synthetic putting green that took up almost all of the small back yard.

Gerry McIlroy, a scratch golfer who'd been a member of Holywood since he was a boy, took on a second job as a bartender at night to raise enough money so he could send his boy to big international tournaments once it was determined Rory was, indeed, that good.

McIlroy used to hit balls for hours from the 17th tee, which is located right outside a clubhouse window. It was just outside that bank of clubhouse windows where McIlroy's remarkable journey to the top of the golf world began.

On a small practice tee next to the 17th tee, McIlroy first started hitting golf balls with Gerry by his side. Now, some 20-plus years later, if these windows could talk, they could have warned the rest of the golf world what McIlroy had in store for it. If those windows could talk...they saw a lot over the years.

"This is where is all started," Gerry McIlroy said, sitting at a clubhouse table sipping a cup of coffee a week before the 2011 British Open. "It seems like yesterday...."

Incredibly, two months after the Masters meltdown, McIlroy won the U.S. Open by eight shots at Congressional Country Club. After he had rebounded from that horrible Masters loss, that win, his first career major championship, would put a stamp on his resilience.

McCormick, the assistant pro at Holywood, said, "We all felt a bit sorry for him at the time on Sunday [of the Masters final round]. Looking back now, and certainly after the U.S. Open, it was a great learning curve for him and even better that it happened to him this early on in his career. He's learned a lot from it and learned a lot about himself as well."

McIlroy later would acknowledge what his close friend McCormick said.

"I learned so much about myself and what I needed to do the next time I got into that position," McIlroy said of that harrowing Masters loss. "If I had not had the whole unravelling, if I had just made a couple of bogeys coming down the stretch and lost by one, I would not have learned as much. Luckily, it did not take me long to get into a position like that again [at the U.S. Open two months later] when I was leading a major and I was able to get over the line quite comfortably. It was a huge learning curve for me and I needed it, and thankfully I have been able to move on to bigger and better things."

McIlroy took the U.S. Open trophy back to his hometown of Holywood, which sits in the shadow of Belfast just 10 minutes east. The day after McIlroy shocked the world with his record-shattering U.S. Open win, the local bakery in town, Skinners, made buns and cupcakes with a clear image in the icing of McIlroy holding the trophy.

"We did it for a day as a novelty and after the first day we said, 'Let's keep doing it,'" Wilson Skinner, the bakery owner, said. "We sold over 4,000 of them."

The irony of McIlroy growing up in Holywood, pronounced the same as Hollywood in California, is he is the furthest thing from the glitz-and-glam type.

To the locals in Holywood, McIlroy will always be that skinny, undersized kid with the freckles and the unruly thatch of brown hair doing otherworldly things with the golf ball since he was old enough to stand on his own two feet.

To a degree, McIlroy's early development as a golfer resulted from his mother, Rosie, working overnight shifts as a production line worker at the local 3M factory making tape. When Rosie returned home from work to sleep, that left Gerry, who started his bartending shift at 6:00 PM, to look after Rory in the mornings.

So he did what any golf-crazed dad would do: he took Rory with him to the golf club and let him watch while he hit balls.

"My earliest memory of Rory was looking out that window and seeing Gerry over at the practice tee on 17 and Rory sitting there while he was looking after him during the day," recalled Gray, the Holywood general manager who grew up playing at the club and worked his way up as the assistant pro and head professional. "As soon as Rory was able to get out of the buggy, he had plastic clubs and was knocking it around the club. It wasn't too long after, when he was three, that he had this little proper golf swing."

Gerry knew early on there was something special about his son's golf skills and focus, saying, "Rory was determined. You just know. Rory always wanted to just get better from when he was a young age."

When Rory reached 8 or 9 years old and needed to travel to competitions around the world, Gerry worked three jobs while his wife worked the overnight shift. They took their vacation time in the summer to bring Rory to tournaments in Hawaii, California, and Florida.

"If we hadn't worked so hard to get the money to send him to those golf tournaments, I could have been sitting back here today asking myself, 'Why didn't I do that?'" Gerry said. "We've been lucky it paid off for him."

Gabby Maguire, who has been running the restaurant and bar concession at Holywood Golf Club since 1998, recalled a Senior Cup match at Holywood, when the custom was to have the players and their opponents announced at a dinner the night before the event. Rory was 13, playing against the best adult players in the club.

"They called out this big guy from the club first and then they announced, 'Rory McIlroy,' and Rory walks out and the guy starts laughing," Maguire said. "[The match] was all over on the 13th. The guy obviously didn't know about Rory back then. I guarantee you that guy's not laughing anymore."

Maguire said he was first taken aback by the magnitude of Rory's fame when the club invited a group of military men from a nearby base to play in a competition. After playing, the servicemen were in the clubhouse for dinner, and McIlroy was playing that evening.

"The guys saw him out the window on the 17th tee box and they stopped eating their meals," Maguire said. "Rory drove the green [356 yards] from the tee box and these guys are watching this. Later, Rory came in and autographed golf balls for the guys, who've been through an awful lot in Afghanistan and Iraq. And they're like kids, melting like putty because they were in the company of Rory McIlroy.

"It was only then when I realized how big Rory is to other people—even though he's still just Rory to us."

Rory's uncle, Colm McIlroy, Gerry's younger brother, remembered taking Rory to a course in Belfast to play every Sunday in the winter. It was him, Gerry, a friend, and Rory.

"He was always miles behind us off the tee, obviously just a wee small fellow," Colm said. "Then one day, when he got to be 13, all of a sudden we're walking up to our drives and there were a couple bunched together and there was one 10 yards ahead. And we're going, 'God, that's Rory.'

"He got to his ball, looked back and said, 'Everything all right back there, guys?' He was only just over 5-foot then."

When Colm saw Rory a few days after his U.S. Open win in 2011, Rory was showing the championship trophy around the club.

"I shook his hand, gave him a hug and I said, 'Well done, Rory. I suppose I can't call you Wee Hacker anymore,'" Colm said. "He said, 'Not for a few weeks, anyway.'"

Despite the great success and wealth McIlroy has already achieved, from the accounts of those who know him best and have observed the way he conducts himself in the public spotlight, the young champion's humble nature might be his best trait.

Gray has heard McIlroy relate how when he was younger, he was just playing golf and not thinking much about the sacrifices his parents made for him.

"But when he looks back now, he realizes his life and his dad and mom's life are so different," Gray said. "I think he appreciates it a lot more now that he's older and gotten to where he's gotten to. He realized he couldn't have gotten there without them. The people around him have obviously had a massive effect on him."

Among those people are his best friends, who remain his closest confidants—McCormick, Tweedie, Paul Dorrian, and Harry Diamond, who's since taken over as McIlroy's caddie.

"Money doesn't matter to Rory," Gerry McIlroy said. "He doesn't change, and I'll tell you why: when he was growing up, we used to say to him, 'The only way to go through life is to be nice. It doesn't cost you any money to be nice.'"

The first thing you notice around Holywood Golf Club is all the young kids toting their carry bags. They all are respectful of the game and visitors, and they make you immediately envision Rory as one of them not long ago.

"They're all buzzing at the moment, excited by it all," Gray, the club general manager, said. "Rory has set a bar, an achievable vision for them, I suppose. Rory has taken the bar from here and put it to the top of the world. They're looking up to the best that any human being can possibly be at golf. They have him as a role model from their own golf club."

Gray described the feeling in Holywood about McIlroy's success as "a mix between just so much pride and disbelief."

"Looking back, everyone expected Rory could do it, but you've got to pinch yourself sometimes to think that the U.S. Open champion came from your little club in Northern Ireland," he said.

Gray paused and looked out those clubhouse windows, as if again envisioning Rory at age two hitting balls on that practice tee with his dad, way back at the beginning of this magical story.

"Looking back on what happened in the 2011 Masters, it doesn't seem as bad when you have four majors on your mantelpiece," McIlroy said. "If I was to look back as a 60-year-old at my career and had not won a green jacket I would be very disappointed. It is the only one left and it is a course I feel I can do well at. I feel I could win multiple times, but getting that first one is the most important thing. Winning all four majors means you are a complete player. I can achieve something special."

———

Tiger Influence

McIlroy was drawn to the game by watching Tiger Woods' record-shattering 12-stroke Masters victory in 1997, and he vowed he would one day do the same.

Among the records the younger McIlroy amassed are becoming the youngest winner of the West of Ireland Championship and the youngest selected for the Walker Cup. At age 16, he set the course record on the demanding Dunluce links at Royal Portrush, where the 2019 British Open was played, in 61. The scorecard is immortalized behind glass doors on the first floor of the clubhouse.

As a nine-year-old, he sent a letter to Woods announcing, "I'm coming to get you. This is the beginning."

McIlroy had just won the 1998 Doral-Publix Junior Golf Classic in Florida for the 10–11 age group, and Woods was the No. 1 ranked player in the world.

"He was someone I put up on a pedestal," McIlroy said of Woods. "Now I obviously have a very different relationship with him. I know him quite well. But I think if you ask a lot of golfers [of] my generation, he was the benchmark. He was the inspiration for us to go out and try to be the best that we could be."

After McIlroy won the world amateur championship and then won his first professional title, in Dubai in 2009, Woods splashed this praise on him: "He's got a lot of talent. We all know he has a lot of talent and it's just a matter of time before he starts winning a bunch of tournaments."

That's exactly what McIlroy has done. By 2019 season's end, he'd won 17 times on the PGA Tour, including his four majors. McIlroy, who pocketed the $15 million prize that came with winning the FedEx Cup Playoffs in the late summer of 2019, has won pretty much everything except a Masters.

And he's insisted that he won't obsess about that or worry about his career being defined by what he hasn't won. McIlroy always has been comfortable in his own skin like that.

"I think there's a difference between a personal desire and a need, and I think I've separated those two," he said. "I would have said a couple of years ago, 'I need to win a Masters. I need a green jacket.' But now it's, 'I want to. I want to win it.' And I'd love to win it. But if I don't, I'm okay. And I think that is the difference.

"I've become comfortable with the fact I've tried four times and I've failed," McIlroy said in advance of the 2019 Masters. "But Abraham Lincoln lost the first 13 elections he was ever in [and] he wound up being the president of the United States. So, I still got a bit of time."

McIlroy's facts on the number of elections Lincoln lost before becoming president of the United States were a little off—it wasn't that many. But his point was made.

"It's definitely taken me time to come to terms with the things I've needed to deal with inside my own head, and I think sometimes I'm too much a fan of the game because I know exactly who has won the Grand Slam and I know exactly the people I would be putting myself alongside," McIlroy said. "So that's maybe a part of [the pressure]. If I didn't know the history of the game and I wasn't such a fan, it would work in my favor. But that's not me.

"[A Grand Slam] would be a massive achievement. It would be huge. But again, I can't think of it that way. I just have to go out and play the golf course the way I know that I can play and repeat that for four days. And as I've said, hopefully that's good enough to have the lowest score that week.

"I feel like I'm good enough to join those people [Sarazen, Hogan, Player, Nicklaus, and Woods], and that it would just be a very proud moment in my life and something that I could look back on, and I would love to sit at the Champions Dinner when I'm 92.

"Believe me, I am motivated to make the most of what I have and to put my name among some of the greats of our game. I'm going to try my ass off there, and I'm probably not going to win. I've had 10 years of learning at Augusta, some tough times. And if one day I'm able to get that green jacket at the end of 72 holes, all of those experiences will have played a part in helping me do that. So, have I a desire to do it? Yes. Do I have a need to do it? No."

Chapter 24

TIGER, 2019

The grill room inside the Augusta National clubhouse was standing-room only on the Sunday afternoon of the 2019 Masters.

Everyone's attention was fixated on two television sets in separate corners of the room, focused on every move Tiger Woods was making on the back nine in what was unfolding into one of the most memorable conclusions in tournament history.

Underneath one of the TVs sat Tiger's family. His mother, Tida, nervously sipped tea. His two children, son Charlie and daughter Sam, noshed on candy, oblivious to the historic goings-on around them. Woods' girlfriend, Erica Herman, was so fidgety that Justin Thomas' mother, Jani, sat down next to her and clutched Herman's right hand as if she was about to give birth.

History hung heavily in the air inside that grill room and around the Augusta National grounds, and it certainly wasn't lost on Woods' loved ones, who were more keenly aware than anyone about the struggle he'd endured to get to this place.

This place: a 15th career major championship, a fifth career green jacket, the end of an 11-year drought without a major and 14 years removed from his last Masters victory.

Something many—including Woods himself—believed would never happen again happened on Sunday at Augusta.

And this one erased a pesky asterisk from Woods' remarkable career resume in that it was the first major championship he's won when trailing entering the final round. Woods already had been lauded as the greatest closer of all time—the Mariano Rivera of his sport. But he'd never chased someone down in a major championship final round.

Until that Sunday.

"Just unreal," Woods would say after overtaking 54-hole leader Francesco Molinari with a frenetic final-round 70 that got him to 13-under par for the week, one better than Brooks Koepka, Dustin Johnson, and Xander Schauffele, and two better than Molinari, who closed with a 74, Jason Day, Webb Simpson, and Tony Finau.

"I had serious doubts after what transpired a couple years ago," Woods said of the four back surgeries he'd endured. "I could barely walk. To have the opportunity to come back like this...it is probably one of the biggest wins I've ever had for sure because of it."

Adding to the sweet taste of this victory was the fact that it was Molinari whom Woods was paired with in the final round at the British Open in July of 2018 at Carnoustie. Woods took the lead on the back nine only to watch the steely and steady diminutive Italian overtake him and hoist the Claret Jug.

This time, the final round turned in favor of Woods and against Molinari on the 12th hole, the par-3 centerpiece of the fabled Amen Corner. For the first 11 holes, there were no signs that Molinari was going to give anything back. He'd been too steady, just like he was at Carnoustie nine months earlier.

And then Molinari pushed his 8-iron tee shot into Rae's Creek on the 12th, took double bogey, and everything changed.

Woods was now tied for the lead at 11-under par and the smell of victory was intoxicating to him—as evidenced by his birdies on 13, 15, and 16, where he came within inches of a hole-in-one, to seize control of the tournament.

"There were so many different scenarios that could have transpired on that back nine," Woods said. "There were so many guys that had a chance to win. The leaderboard was absolutely packed and everyone was playing well. You couldn't have had more drama than we all had out there, and now I know why I'm balding. This stuff is hard."

The birdie on No. 13 gave Woods his first final-round Masters lead since 2005, the last time he'd been fitted for a green jacket.

"It didn't feel unfamiliar because I had the lead at the Open Championship, so that was just two majors ago," Woods said. "I just kept saying, 'I've been here, it wasn't that long ago. Just go ahead and just keep playing your game, keep plodding along and keep doing all the little things correctly.'"

The birdie on 16 gave Woods a two-shot lead and Augusta National, which is a place of decorum—where fans are called "patrons" and no running is permitted on the grounds—was off the rails.

"I birdied 13, I birdied 15 with two good shots in there, and almost whooped it at 16," Woods said. "That gave me the cushion, and I kept telling myself on 17, that tee shot, I said, 'I've been in this position before. I had a two-shot lead with [Chris] DiMarco and went bogey, bogey [in 2005]. Let's go ahead and pipe this ball right down the middle.' I hit a little flat squeezer out there and I did, I just smoked it.

"Then on 18, I said, 'Hey, it's not over yet. Arnold [Palmer] once lost the tournament and lost the hole with a double. So let's keep the hammer down. Brooksy could still make birdie up 18 and I could make bogey and next thing you know we're in a playoff, so let's get this ball in play.' I did that, and I saw [Koepka] tap out for par [on 18], and that gave me the cushion knowing that I could make bogey."

Which he did, which was enough to win comfortably.

"I just felt so prepared coming into this event," Woods said. "This year, my finishes don't really reflect it, but I was starting to shape the golf ball the way that I know I can, which I needed for this week. Prep for the Masters started six months ago, so just trying to make sure I get ready to peak for this one week, and I did, and everything came together, which is great.

"I kept doing all the little things correctly. Missed the ball in the correct spots time and time and time again, and if I was out of position, so be it, take my bogey and move on. I had no doubles this week. Just kept, as I said, just kept plodding along."

By the time he plodded off the 18th green, suddenly, one of the world's most famous and snooty golf clubs felt a lot more like Yankee Stadium with fans chanting, "Tiger, Tiger, Tiger," as Woods fell into the arms first of his caddie, Joe LaCava; then his son, Charlie, whom he squeezed so tightly you worried for the child's health; then his daughter, Sam, with whom he had a long, emotional embrace; then Herman.

"It hasn't sunk in at all," Woods said afterward. "It's going to take a little bit of time."

Woods has said for the past couple of years that his biggest motivation was to win a major in front of his children now that they're old enough to understand the magnitude of the moments. He said all they'd associated golf with was the pain it had been causing their dad.

That Sunday was the first time Charlie and Sam had been to Augusta National, the place where Woods formally introduced himself to the world with his record-shattering victory in 1997.

"I hope they are proud of me," Woods said. "I hope they are proud of their dad. I've been very blessed to have two great kids, and just to have them here to see this and witness this...they have never been to Augusta National. This is a pretty unique event. This is very special. So it all worked out and here they are."

When Woods first started winning majors early in his career, his father, Earl, was a staple waiting for him at the 18th green for a congratulatory hug. By the late '90s, though, Earl's health began to deteriorate before he died in 2006. Earl was there in 1997 for his son's first Masters win for a tearful hug as Woods walked off of the 18th.

"My dad's no longer here, but my mom's here, 22 years later, and I happen to win the tournament," Woods said. "And then to have both Sam and Charlie here, they were there at the British Open last year when I had the lead on that back nine and I made a few mistakes, cost myself a chance to win The Open title.

"I wasn't going to let that happen to them twice," Woods said with a smile. "So, for them to see what it's like to have their dad win a major championship, I hope that's something they will never forget. I think the kids are starting to understand how much this game means to me, and some of the things I've done in the game. Prior to [the] comeback, they only knew that golf caused me a lot of pain. If I tried to swing a club I would be on the ground and I struggled for years, and that's basically all they remember. We're creating new memories for them, and it's just very special."

Woods said having his kids there to see him win "means the world to me."

"Their love and their support, I just can't say enough how much that meant to me throughout my struggles when I really just had a hard time moving around," he said. "Just their infectiousness of happiness [while] I was going through a tough time physically...there were a lot of times when I really couldn't move, and so that in itself is difficult. But just to have them there, and then now to have them see their Pops win, just like my Pops saw me win here, it's pretty special.

"This whole tournament has meant so much to me over the years. Coming here in '95 for the first time and being able to play as an amateur, winning in '97 and then come full circle, 22 years later, to be able to do it again, and just the way it all transpired and to have my family is something I'll never, ever forget."

———

Peers' Reaction

As euphoric as the patrons around the grounds were, the reaction of Woods' fellow competitors was astounding.

"I'm just ecstatic for golf and I'm ecstatic for Tiger," Zach Johnson, the 2007 Masters winner, said. "We just witnessed history. It's raw, it's fresh, we're 10 minutes after the fact, so hear me out: I don't know what a better comeback in sports is. I'm sure there are probably ones you can argue. But in my lifetime, I don't think I've seen a comeback like this."

Woods' peers, all of them years younger than him and all of them inspired to become pros because of him, gathered at the clubhouse after Woods had put the finishing touches on his fifth career Masters win and first since 2005, first major championship win since 2008.

Rickie Fowler was there, along with Justin Thomas, Bubba Watson, Brooks Koepka, Xander Schauffele, and Johnson, to name a few. Even two-time Masters winner Bernhard Langer was there to witness it and congratulate Woods.

"I saw light at the end of the tunnel," Fowler said of Woods breaking through to win another major after the long, agonizing wait that included the multiple back surgeries, an addiction to pain-killers that landed him in rehab after a DUI arrest, not to mention his embarrassing infidelity scandal that very publicly ended his marriage. "I saw this as something that potentially could happen. I also knew the 15th major was going to be the hardest. Seeing how healthy he was and how much fun he was having playing the game a couple falls ago when we were at home, he had plenty to go win.

"I don't doubt that this is going to be his most special one...yet. To get his 15th after a long wait, after a lot of years away from competitive golf to be in position where he wasn't sure if he'd be able to play again...it's cool stuff."

Thomas, who, like Fowler, plays a lot of golf with Woods in the Jupiter, Florida, area where they all live, also said he expected Woods to rise again in majors.

"I've played enough with him and know that he was playing well enough and I thought the final round was going to be big in how he handled it," Thomas said. "He's been there a lot, been there more than anybody, but it had been a while since he'd been there here, had a chance to win here. Whether he admits it or not, I'm sure this one is one of the most important or biggest [wins]."

Even Molinari, whom Woods vanquished on that final round back nine, sounded genuinely happy for the winner.

"It's great to see Tiger doing well, but the way he was playing last year I think we all knew it was coming sooner or later," Molinari said. "So maybe next time it will be better for me, but it was nice to be out with him. He played well, he hit the right shots at the right time and deserved to win."

Tony Finau, who was also in the final group with Woods, said the day before the final round that Woods' 1997 Masters win was the reason he took up golf. As he spoke, Finau held his young son in his arms and was asked what he'll tell him about the experience when he's old enough to understand.

"I'll tell him I was there in the final group when Tiger won his 15th major," Finau said. "At that point, I'll hopefully have a few under my own belt. This is something that I've dreamed of for a long time. I'm going to relish in the moment and enjoy being in contention at a Masters. As a kid, I always wanted to compete against him and have the opportunity of playing in the final group with him in a major championship.

"You can't say enough about Tiger and what he's done for the game. It's great for him to be involved in the game and now he's got his 15th major. He's going to be a force to be reckoned with these next few years, I'm sure."

Finau, speaking with the breathless enthusiasm of a kid who'd just gotten off his first thrill ride at an amusement park, called it "fun being a part of the action" as a part of the Woods final-round vortex.

"You can't beat the experience," he said. "It's something you can't pay for. When you're someone like me in my shoes still trying to come up, still trying to win majors, still trying to contend, you can't beat playing with the best player in the world, the best that's ever done it and just see if you can get the job done is cool. I wanted to get the job done, but Tiger is great for the game and again, unbelievable that he's winning his 15th major today.

"It was a lot of fun to be in that type of atmosphere. It's what I practice for, what I play for, what I train for. My time is coming. I know it is. I've just got to keep riding the storm."

Even in defeat as he searched for his first career major championship, Schauffele called that final round "an awesome experience."

"What I witnessed, I know it's what everyone is going to talk about for a long time," he said. "It was really cool coming down the stretch, all the historic holes, Amen Corner, 15, 16, Tiger making the roars. I was trying to push myself, but I feel like I got a very full, fully filled Masters experience here in my second year.

"With what we just witnessed with Tiger coming off 18, it was a throwback, seeing him in red in the mock turtleneck. It's what I saw as a kid, and it was just really cool to know him a little bit now and congratulate him coming off 18."

Brooks Koepka, one of the three runners-up to finish one shot behind Woods, said he was "happy for Tiger, after everything that's gone on, and it's cool to see."

"This is definitely probably one of the greatest comebacks I think anybody's ever seen," Koepka said. "That was probably the coolest back nine in a major championship I've ever been a part of. I don't know how it looked on TV, but it was amazing to be a part of. It was quite fun. I watch the leaderboard all the time to see where guys are at and what they are doing, and to see Tiger, what he did down the stretch was impressive. We already knew he was back, but I think he put the exclamation point on it.

"I think we all knew [another major] was going to come. I said it [in 2018] at the British, I thought he was ready, raring to go to win a major again and it only took him, what, two more tries? It's impressive, it's fun to watch and it's, as a fan, just of golf and of Tiger, it's very special. To be able to come back out here and have the Tiger of old back, as a fan, I love it. I'm glad he's back.

"It's probably one of the coolest things to be a part of it, even though I finished second place [and am] a little bummed out. But I wouldn't want it any other way. You want to play against the best to ever play. You want to go toe-to-toe with them. I enjoy the battle, I enjoy everything that goes on with it. It's what I watched as a kid. It's what I watched growing up.

"It was an incredible experience. He got the better of me this time. I'm sure he's ecstatic about it, but hopefully there will be a few more."

Eight months earlier, at the PGA Championship at Bellerive in St. Louis, Koepka staved off a furious Woods rally in the final round to win. It was there Koepka got his first true taste of Tigermania.

"The atmosphere around Tiger is mind-blowing, and to be inside the ropes and just kind of see it as another player is pretty cool and unique," Koepka said. "I heard it at the PGA. You hear it here [at Augusta]. You know any time he does something good, the fans are going to get excited and they are going to be loud, and that's the following that he's created. It's cool to see if you take a step back while you're playing. I mean, you watch him walk down after he won on 18 there, I mean, it was just a monsoon of people. It's incredible."

———

Turning Point

Amen Corner, one of the most storied and sacred grounds in golf, isn't famous for no reason. So it should come as no surprise that the par-3 12th hole, the centerpiece of Amen Corner, had a lot to say about the final outcome of the 2019 Masters.

Everything changed on the 12th hole Sunday. For Woods. For Molinari. For Koepka. And for Finau. The latter three hit their tee shots into Rae's Creek. Woods did not.

Four players in the last two groupings found the water off the tee at the 12th, including Molinari, who was two shots ahead of Woods at the time. Finau, also in contention and playing along with Woods and Molinari, also found the water and so did Koepka, who was in the group ahead of Woods.

All of them took damaging double bogeys on the hole, while Woods managed a par and never looked back from there on his way to victory.

Woods walked to the 13th tee tied with Molinari at 11-under, while Koepka went from 11-under to 9-under and Finau went from 10-under to 8-under.

Woods promptly birdied the par-5 13th to take the lead, the first time he had a final-round lead in the Masters since 2005, and he never let go of it.

"That mistake Francesco made there let a lot of guys back into the tournament, myself included," Woods said. "There were so many different scenarios that could have transpired on that back nine. There were so many guys that had a chance to win. The leaderboard was absolutely packed and everyone was playing well."

Molinari lamented a poorly-executed 8-iron for his missed shot at the 12.

"I think we picked the right shot and just didn't hit it hard enough," he said. "It was tough with the wind gusting. I managed to scramble well on the front nine. I just had a couple of mental lapses on the back nine that were costly. I think it wasn't my day today. That ball on 12, if it's one yard farther left it probably goes in the bunker.

"Obviously, I did a couple of things that I wish I had done differently. But I'll learn from my mistakes."

Molinari had bogeyed No. 11 in the first round and then went 49 holes without a blemish on his card until he got to the 12th on Sunday.

"It was probably 9-iron yardage, but I didn't want the wind to gust and get the ball too much," he said. "I just didn't hit it hard enough. Sometimes it's your day. Sometimes it isn't."

Finau conceded that the 12th hole, which with some swirling winds played as the most difficult hole on the course with a cumulative scoring average of 3.38, was the turning point.

"For me 12 was the turning point, that was the tournament," Finau said. "It's a hard shot. Not my best swing and it ended up costing me. Francesco had just hit it in the water, and I knew I just had to hit it on land. It was the perfect club for me. I barely hit it chunky and it kind of rolled on me. The line was okay, and I thought it had a chance to fly on the green and unfortunately it didn't.

"I knew from then on I had to play pretty much perfect golf. I still could have made something happen down the stretch. But 12 was kind of a big swing."

Koepka blamed a gust of wind for his water ball on 12, saying, "Once it gets above those trees, it's just a guessing game."

Woods?

"All I was concentrating on was I had 147 over the first tongue in the bunker there, and so my number, I was hitting it 150 and just be committed to hitting it 150," he said. "I saw Brooksy ended up short. Poults [Ian Poulter] ended up short, as well. So when I was up there on the tee box and it was about my turn to go, I could feel that wind puff up a little bit.

"Brooksy is stronger than I am and he flights it better than I do, so I'm sure he hit 9-iron and didn't make it. So I knew my 9-iron couldn't cover the flag, so I had to play left, and I said, 'Just be committed, hit it over that tongue in that bunker. Let's get out of here and let's go handle the par-5s.' And I did."

Woods, by far the most experienced of the players in contention, credited his experience for helping him make No. 12 the turning point in the round.

"It helps being around here and playing this golf course so many different times," he said.

Molinari's caddie Pello Iguaran perhaps captured the consequences of No. 12 and what it meant for Woods best when he said, "You cannot open the door to those kinds of great players. So you see what happens."

———

Moving Day

There's an unmistakable energy that engulfs a golf tournament—particularly a major championship—when Woods is merely in the field. The crowds are exponentially larger. The buzz on the grounds is palpable.

That energy when Woods is in contention to win a major is another story entirely. There are few things in sports like it. Think Super Bowls and heavyweight championship fights.

This is the high-voltage electricity that would grip Augusta National for Sunday's final round with Woods playing in the final group, two shots out of the lead held by Molinari.

The man Woods needed to run down and catch was the unflappable, steely-nerved Italian whom he failed to overtake the previous July at Carnoustie, where Molinari won the British Open despite Woods having taken the lead on the back nine in the final round.

Molinari and Woods were paired together and Molinari stared Woods down, didn't show as much as a quiver of intimidation as he, not Woods, hoisted the Claret Jug.

Molinari, who shot 66 in the third round and was 13-under par, again played with Woods in the final round, joined by Finau, who like Woods was 11-under par.

Koepka, winner of two of the previous three majors, was 10-under. Simpson and Ian Poulter were 9-under.

When it was pointed out to Woods on Saturday that he had a chance and that this was the closest he'd been to winning a green jacket in years, he said, "That was the plan and here I am."

"It's been a while since I've been in contention here," Woods said. "But then again, the last two majors count for something. I've been in the mix with a chance to win major championships [the British Open and PGA Championship] in the last two years. So that helps."

As it turned out, it would.

"If he brings the game he had today, we're going to see what kind of Tiger effect there is on this generation," David Duval said on the Golf Channel after that Saturday round. "Look at his eyes: they look like they did 10, 12 years ago. There's an intensity and also an ease with what he's doing."

––––––––

Unlikely Comeback

Not long before that magical week in Georgia, Woods was not sure he'd ever be anywhere close to at his best again. What he would accomplish that Masters week felt unfathomable, unrealistic, impossible.

Two years earlier, Woods thought his career was over after the third back surgery didn't relieve his pain. But spinal fusion surgery on April 19, 2017, gave him a new lease on life, and golf.

On the eve of that Masters, during the Golf Writers Association of America's annual awards dinner, Woods was the recipient of the GWAA's Ben Hogan Award, given to the player who "has overcome a physical handicap or serious injury to remain active in golf."

"Golf was not in my near future or even distant future," Woods told the audience that Wednesday night before the opening round of the 83rd Masters. "I knew I was going to be part of the game, but playing the game, I couldn't even do that with my son Charlie. I couldn't putt in the backyard. But playing the game again? I was done at that particular time."

Woods' back issues were so dire that he nearly wasn't even able to make it to the Masters Champions Dinner in 2017, even though he was unable to play in the tournament. He revealed that he had to take a pain-relieving "nerve blocker" injection just to be at Augusta for the dinner.

"I got there and didn't want to miss it," Woods said. "It was tough and uncomfortable."

It was at that dinner where Woods quietly confided to some people that he didn't think he was ever going to play again.

"I know he whispered to another Masters champion two Masters dinners ago [in 2017], 'I'm done. I won't play golf again,' and here we are, 18 months later," said Nick Faldo, a two-time Masters champion and current golf broadcaster who was at that dinner.

Woods recalled that the day after that 2017 Champions Dinner he flew to England to see a back specialist, who recommended that he undergo a spinal fusion. Woods decided to go through with the procedure, and it saved his career—and his life as a normal functioning human being.

"It was not a fun time and a tough couple of years there," Woods said. "But I was able to start to walk again, I was able to participate in life, I was able to be around my kids again and go to their games, go to their practices, take them to school again. These are all things I couldn't do for a very long time."

Woods wasn't able to make a full swing with a driver until September 2017 at the Presidents Cup in New Jersey, where he served as a non-playing vice captain. And even then, he joked that his first few drives traveled only 90 yards.

At the '19 Masters, Woods led the field in greens hit in regulation (83 percent) largely because he drove the ball so beautifully.

"It's the best I've felt with a driver in years," Woods said. "I was able to hit the golf ball both ways this week, and some of the shots I hit down 13, turn it around the corner, a couple of drives down 2, some of the bombs I hit down 3; and then to hit little squeezers out there down 7; you saw it today on 15 and 17 and even on 18, just little trap squeezers out there, as well.

"I was able to hit both ends of the spectrum, low cuts and high draws. That's not easy to do, so I just really felt that I had that much control in my long game and it paid off."

After he won, Twitter blew up with high-profile celebrity congratulations to Woods.

From former president Barack Obama: "Congratulations, Tiger! To come back and win the Masters after all the highs and lows is a testament to excellence, grit, and determination."

From former president Donald Trump: "Watching final hole of @TheMasters. @TigerWoods is looking GREAT!"

Another from Trump: "Love people who are great under pressure. What a fantastic life comeback for a really great guy!"

From former New England Patriots quarterback Tom Brady, who's won six Super Bowls: "Running the numbers on how long it'll take me to get to 15…"

From Golden State Warriors star Stephen Curry: "Greatest comeback story in sports."

From tennis star Serena Williams: "I am literally in tears watching @TigerWoods this is Greatness like no other....I am so inspired thank you buddy."

Woods finished 13-under 275 for the week and became, at age 43, the oldest Masters champion since Nicklaus won his sixth green jacket at 46 in 1986. Woods' fifth Masters title moved him past Arnold Palmer and put him one behind Nicklaus for the most green jackets in history. Woods made his debut in 1995 and was the low amateur. He went on to win in 1997, 2001, 2002, 2005, and then 2019.

Woods, who had gone 28 majors over 11 years without winning before that 2019 Masters, set or tied 27 records when he won the 1997 Masters by 12 shots, including being the youngest winner at 21 years, three months, which still stands. Now he owns the record for length of time between Masters victories at 14 years. Nicklaus has the record for the length between the first victory and his last one, at 23 years. Woods went 22 years between his first and fifth wins.

"A big 'well done' from me to Tiger," Nicklaus tweeted. "I am so happy for him and for the game of golf. This is just fantastic!!!"

Fred Ridley, the chairman of Augusta National Golf Club and the Masters Tournament, called the final round "an epic Sunday and a great day for golf," adding, "It's one of the most amazing days in our history."

"Tiger, welcome back," Masters media chairman Craig Heatley, his voice cracking, said in his New Zealand accent as he introduced Woods in the post-round press conference. "Or should I say, more appropriately, welcome home."

———

18 in Play?

Golf is a numbers game. You try to shoot a number. You try to beat a number. The golf course has 18 holes and you try to conquer each of them.

After Woods' 2019 Masters victory, the newest, most relevant number for him again became 18—as in his pursuit of Nicklaus' record of 18 career major championship victories was back in play.

There was that time, back in the late '90s and early 2000s, when Woods was mowing down major championships, checking off boxes and ruthlessly moving on to the next thing. After his 2008 U.S. Open victory, the 11 years that followed without a major championship victory for Woods felt like an eternity for him and it felt like the end for the rest of us wondering whether he'd win another one. He was stuck on 14 majors and it seemed like that was going to be where the number stood forever—second to Nicklaus' 18.

And then the 2019 Masters happened.

It seemed like it hadn't been 10 minutes after Woods' final putt disappeared into the cup on No. 18 at Augusta and he hugged his family and friends greenside when everyone was ready to re-start the Woods–Nicklaus countdown.

"This keeps 18 in play," Fowler said, standing outside the clubhouse with Masters patrons still chanting Woods' name.

"Eighteen is, I think, a lot closer than people think," Koepka said. "I would say that's probably what all fans...what we're thinking—that he's definitely back and 18's not far."

Woods, after his first Masters win since 2005 and first major championship since 2008, was asked if he thought Nicklaus "should be worried" about Woods catching him.

"I don't know if he's worried or not," Woods said. "I'm sure he's home in West Palm just chilling and watching."

Can Woods win more majors?

Of course, he can.

Will he?

The chances improved greatly after Masters 2019.

If you don't think he'll be one of the favorites to win more Masters for the foreseeable future, you didn't pay enough attention to what transpired in April 2019, and specifically in that final round.

Nicklaus, in an interview on the Golf Channel the night of Woods' victory, said, "I don't ever pull against anybody. Nobody wants their record to be broken. But I certainly wouldn't want Tiger to be hurt and not to be able to do it. Of course, he is now pretty healthy and playing well. I wish him well. I always wish the guys well and I want them to play their best and don't want anybody to play poorly."

Nicklaus said as he watched Woods play the final round, he thought, "This is a man who is possessed. He is possessed to win the golf tournament. He absolutely under total control and he was going to get it done. There wasn't any question in my mind after seeing Molinari hit the ball in the water at 12 and Tiger put it on the green. I said, 'The tournament is over. It doesn't make any difference what anybody else is going to do. Somebody else is going to make mistakes, but Tiger is not going to make any.' And he didn't.

"You watch how smart he played and how he used his head at 12 and he put the ball in the middle of the green," Nicklaus went on. "How he put the ball to the left of the pin at 13. How he put the ball in the middle of the green at 14 and 15. How he put the ball to the right of the hole at 16 to use the slope. Right on the middle of the green at 17.

"What a nice, smart pitch shot on 18. He hit the pitch shot so it wouldn't roll through the green. He hit the pitch shot into the slope so it would come back. Every shot I saw him play was a smart shot. When you've got a guy who plays smart shots like that, plays them well and knows what he's doing and plays them with confidence, he should be your winner.

"I think he understands who he is, understands how to play the game, understands how to play smart, and how to play where you are not going to put yourself in a position to play bad. Tiger has been a terrible driver the past few years. He drove the ball magnificent [in the final round]."

Nicklaus added, "Everybody has been asking me about Tiger, 'Can Tiger win again? Will he win another major?' I thought for a long time that he was going to win again."

Asked if that win refocused his sights on getting to 18 majors, Woods said, "I really haven't thought about that yet. I'm sure that I'll probably think of it going down the road, but right now it's a little soon. I'm just enjoying 15."

Woods' caddie, Joe LaCava, also was not about to get ahead of himself.

"Before this, I never thought about 18 for him; I just thought about 15," LaCava said. "Now that he has 15, we'll think about 16. I always think the sky's the limit for the guy, but I don't think of 18 as a caddie. It's been a long time for him, a lot of question marks, injuries. Yeah, 10 years from now looking back, No. 15 probably was the hardest one for him to win."

Woods' biggest takeaway from the win was this: "I can win majors now," he said.

When he won the Tour Championship in September of 2018 at East Lake to end a five-year winless drought, Woods said that showed him he could win again. It all sounded so difficult to believe for a player who'd won 79 times, including 14 majors, at that time. But confidence is a fragile being, and even the greatest in the world needs a shot of it every once in a while for reinforcement.

"The win at East Lake was a big confidence booster for me because I had come close last year a couple times and I didn't quite do it," Woods said. "East Lake was a big step for me, confirming that I could still win out here and against the best players. My last three major championships have been pretty good, so that in itself gives me a lot of confidence going down the road."

Woods' Masters triumph left you to wonder whether his fellow players, the same players who gushed about his win at Augusta, unwittingly fell into a trap.

In the years that Woods struggled to find his game that won him that fifth green jacket, the younger generation of golfers who grew up watching him dominate and intimidate pined to have the chance to compete against him while he was playing like the major-championship-winning Tiger of old.

That magical week at Augusta, particularly in the final round, they got their wish. That begged the question: Should these players be careful what they wished for?

Woods, en route to winning that 15th career major and fifth Masters to end an 11-year drought without a major and 14 years since his last Masters victory, left those of that very younger generation in his wake on his way to the Butler Cabin to collect his fifth green jacket.

Is this an omen of things to come for Woods—and his current crop of competitors—now that he's broken through and proven to himself that he can resume winning majors again?

Back in his days of dominance, Woods broke the spirit of some of his nearest competitors while he was collecting his first 14 major championships.

Ernie Els, a perpetual major championship bridesmaid to Woods, was left baffled, frustrated, and at his wits' end. David Duval, who for a short period wrested the No. 1 world ranking from Woods, didn't last very long before his desire to compete for majors burned out. Vijay Singh took his lumps from Woods. How many more wins would Phil Mickelson have had it not been for his prime coinciding with that of Woods?

"The first golf tournament I ever watched was the '97 Masters," Finau said. "Just watching Tiger dominate the way that he did was very inspiring for me for some reason as a kid, and I took up the game the summer of '97, I think in huge part because of Tiger. Tiger taught us how to compete.

"We're the aftermath, if you will, of the 'Tiger Effect.' The way he dominated and watching him growing up, it was like he was scared of nobody. So, I think a lot of us try to be like him and try to be that way to where nothing on the golf course can scare us and our skills can showcase. He's playing against a different generation now. He's playing against guys that he kind of bred.

"We were watching him as teenagers through high school and watching him dominate, and I think all of us relish now having a chance to compete against him."

In the end on that final-round Sunday, it didn't work out so well for Finau. He hit his approach shot into Rae's Creek on the par-3 12th hole, as did Molinari, the leader at the time, gifting Woods a tie for that lead with double bogeys.

One hole later, a Woods birdie on 13, and he was in the lead he would never relinquish. Three holes after that, Woods birdied No. 16 to take a two-shot lead and the final two holes were a formality.

For those who followed Woods "back in the day," this was a familiar scene. Once he got the lead the tournament was over.

Did Woods' presence—the Tiger Effect—have any influence over how those players in contention around him failed to perform at their peak when the heat of pressure began to rise?

There's no tangible way to measure these things. But Finau did concede that a Tiger Effect remains in existence.

"I stay in my lane and do my thing no matter who I'm playing with, but there's always a Tiger Effect, no matter who you are," Finau said. "I'm not going to act like it's not there, because I know that it is."

For some of the younger players, like Schauffele, the experience around Woods is still a novelty. As such, he sounded a lot more thrilled at Woods breaking through to win his 15th major than he sounded devastated that he wasn't able to win his first.

"It's hard to really feel bad about how I played...because I just witnessed history," Schauffele said. "It's what I watched as a kid. It was like a dream, honestly."

Yes, but if Woods turns this Masters victory into another one of his historical runs through majors, that dream will turn into a nightmare for the likes of Schauffele, Finau, Fowler, Bryson DeChambeau, and the other young players who are seeking their first major championship if they keep getting denied by their idol the way he denied the likes of Els, Duval, Singh, and Mickelson for all those years.

It, too, could affect those who've already broken through to win majors but crave more.

"I'm sure he feels like he has a great chance," Justin Thomas, a one-time major winner, said of Woods' chase of Nicklaus' record of 18 majors. "More importantly, I hope I can do something to stop it."

Chapter 25

THE CADDIE

The very essence of who Joe LaCava is can be captured in the 15 frenetic seconds of Tiger Woods' celebration that immediately followed his fifth career Masters victory in April 2019.

Look at the TV clip: there's no immediate sign of LaCava in the frame while Woods wildly releases 11 years of frustration without a major championship victory with a series of emotional fist pumps and arms and putter thrust toward the sky.

When LaCava finally enters the frame, with Woods seeking him out for an embrace, Woods jubilantly screams to his caddie, "We did it!"

"No," LaCava responded to Woods. "You did it."

This is who LaCava is to his core. He's a background guy, not a "me" guy. Woods' former caddie, Steve Williams, who authored some of the most awkwardly misjudged high fives in sports history, always celebrated Woods' victories as if he was the one who had been making the shots. There always was an air of self-importance about Williams.

LaCava is about everything but self-importance

"I didn't put in all the hard work, I didn't have all the surgeries, I wasn't down in Florida grinding," LaCava said after

Woods' Masters win. "So, for me, it's easy. I just show up, try to do a halfway decent job and he has to do all the tough work."

That's not entirely true. It was LaCava who texted Woods days before they were to meet at Augusta to practice before the tournament began. He implored Woods to get to the course early Sunday to walk the holes with only a wedge and a putter to work on his short game, because that's what LaCava felt needed some last-minute work.

Woods later would credit LaCava for his prescience, citing how much his short game helped him win a fifth green jacket.

It was also LaCava calming down and pumping up Woods with some powerful words on the first tee of the final round. "Intense but loose," LaCava told him. "Don't carry the weight of the world on your shoulders."

Then it was LaCava giving Woods a stern talking-to after a second consecutive bogey on the fifth hole, a message that helped turn Woods' round around.

"The talk that Joey and I had off of 5—I just listened," Woods recalled. "Then I went into the restroom and proceeded to say the same things over and over to myself, and then came out and I felt a lot better."

LaCava is so much more than a "keep-up-and-shut-up" caddie toting Woods' bag around the golf course. He's an integral, trusted part of Woods' success and he's become a close friend, too, since they hooked up in 2011.

LaCava is a 55-year-old lifer in golf whose fierce loyalties are unbreakable, whether it's his rooting interest in the Giants and Rangers or his work with Woods.

LaCava, who wore a New York Giants running back Saquon Barkley T-shirt under his white caddie overalls during the final round at Augusta National last month, could have left Woods to work for another player at any time during the two years Woods was effectively sidelined with back surgeries. During one stretch when Woods' back limited him most, LaCava went 466 days without working.

Woods encouraged him to work for another player.

"He was suggesting to me—at least giving me the option—to go work for someone else," LaCava said. "He knows that I like to work and want to work, he knows how competitive I am and how much I do enjoy caddying. He also said, 'If you latch onto somebody full-time and you guys are hitting it off and doing very well together, I've got no problem if you go off riding into the sunset with that guy, and I hope it works out for you.'"

LaCava never considered it, choosing to ride it out until Woods would become healthy enough to compete again—despite how dire it looked at times.

LaCava, who's been with Woods for 10 wins, called Woods' loyalty to him "the same as I've been to him, if not more."

"He looked after me financially when he was out," LaCava said. "He'd send me some nice texts to check on me and my family when he was not playing for a long time. He also expressed, 'If you don't move on [to another player], terrific, I want to have you and I hope you stick around. I want you as my caddie when I do come back.' That meant a lot to me when I was sitting out."

The wait for LaCava has been well worth it. Woods' win at Augusta was a second career major championship for LaCava, who was on Fred Couples' bag when he won the Masters in 1992.

Perhaps the most emotional moment for LaCava and Woods came while they were in the scorer's room minutes after the 2019 win at Augusta.

"We just kind of looked at each other and soaked it all in," LaCava recalled. "We just took a deep breath. Nothing was really said. We got to share the moment and smile at each other. It was such an achievement, a proud moment more than anything.

Nothing needed to be said because we could read each other's minds."

LaCava said Woods later sent him a text message that read, "We did it, appreciate you hanging in there with me, I love you like a brother."

The byproducts of the Woods victory have been plentiful, including countless text messages from the likes of Chris Mara from the Giants, former Giants tight end Mark Bavaro, and former New York Rangers Brad Richards and Martin St. Louis, with whom LaCava is close.

"These are guys that I was watching on TV and respect the heck out of and now they're reaching out to me because they love golf," LaCava said.

LaCava has been a staple at Augusta National for some 30 years. The Connecticut native and lifer caddie has been with Woods for the bulk of Woods' attempted comeback, and he'd endured much of the heartache with Woods.

That 2019 Masters win, Woods' first major championship victory since 2008 and first Masters win since 2005, was a momentous occasion for both player and caddie.

"I'm just happy for him winning, because this one might have bought me a couple more months," LaCava said with his signature self-deprecation.

LaCava has become like family to Woods, often staying with him on his yacht (named Privacy) during tournament weeks and hanging out with him at his home in South Florida. LaCava is probably as paramount in importance to Woods' comeback as anyone.

The scene on No. 18 at Augusta with the crowd going bananas and Woods' mother, two children, and girlfriend waiting for him on the back of the green?

"It was a special moment," LaCava said. "He was typical Tiger. He said, 'We did it,' and I said, 'No, you did it. You played great.' Very special. I knew his kids were out here, so I thought that was even more special."

There was that moment before tournament week when LaCava quietly urged Woods to tweak his preparation routine, and that advice might have been a catalyst to the victory.

"[The previous week] I texted him and said, 'How about we get up there on Sunday afternoon with nobody around and chip and putt on one of the nines?'" LaCava recalled. "At that time, I thought that was the part of his game that needed the most work. I could tell once he took that to heart, he was like, 'I've got to work on my short game a little more and I've got to get after it.'"

LaCava, not the outward emotional type, described Woods as "pretty emotional and pretty jacked up" after the win.

"He thinks in the back of his mind that a lot of people doubted him," LaCava said. "I don't look at it that way. He's not trying to prove people wrong. He's just happy that he won."

As LaCava spoke in the aftermath of the Woods victory, he was leaning on the back of Woods' courtesy car, in which he'd just put the 18th pin and flag.

"I've got to get off the property before I get arrested," he joked.

He talked about his own feelings, about the reward for him sticking it out for so long with Woods when it looked so grim.

"I was sitting around thinking, 'This sucks sitting at home,'" LaCava said. "But it was all worth it."

The 2019 Masters was LaCava's first major while working with Woods. The only other major championship he'd won before in his career was that '92 Masters with Couples.

"I didn't want to be a caddie for only one guy that won a major," LaCava said. "I don't know if I dreamt about it, but I pictured it. I don't think I would have stuck around for as long as I did if I didn't think he wasn't capable of pulling something like this off. I mean, he is Tigers Woods after all, right?"

LaCava, as regular a guy as you'll find in the game, player or caddie, has played a big part in humanizing Woods, who had spent so much of his career building a reputation as untouchable, cold and aloof, and above it all.

"He's high-fiving people, talking to people, signing some autographs," LaCava said. "I think he's enjoying playing golf and being around people. He's much more fan-friendly, great with the kids. Everyone out there is pulling for him. He's enjoying it more."

A month after Woods' Masters victory, he was invited to the White House by president Donald Trump to be given a Presidential Medal of Freedom. LaCava and his wife, Megan, were invited by Woods to be a part of his small gathering of those closest to him.

"I wasn't surprised [to be invited], but certainly appreciative of the fact that my name was on the list and the list was somewhat small, and to include my wife as well was great," LaCava said. "He makes my whole family feel a part of the team, so that's a great thing for me. I feel fortunate to have the job that I have. I love working for the guy. I'm not going anywhere."

EPILOGUE

I t was never going to be the same.
Not in 2020.

The 2020 Masters was unlike the 83 of them that preceded it. It will forever be known as the COVID-19 Masters.

There were no patrons allowed onto the grounds at Augusta National because of safety protocols necessitated by the pandemic. That left an emptiness to the tournament, which was devoid of those distinctive electric roars that rattle through the tall pines from grandstand to grandstand when players are carding birdies and eagles throughout the week—particularly on the back nine of the Sunday final round.

Walking around the grounds and not seeing patrons lining the fairways, cramming the grandstands, jamming the merchandise building, and eating pimento cheese and egg salad sandwiches and sipping Masters Punches from the signature plastic logoed cups was surreal.

A limited number of media were allowed into the event in 2020, maybe 10 percent of the usual mass that covers the event internationally. Other than tournament officials, players, caddies, and media, the only people allowed on the grounds included members and a "plus-one" guest. Players, too, were allowed one guest, usually a spouse or partner.

Because of the light crowds, the celebrities in the midst were more exposed, as NFL commissioner Roger Goodell (an Augusta member) and his wife strolled the grounds with former NFL quarterback Peyton Manning (also a member), along with Major League Baseball commissioner Rob Manfred.

The 2020 Masters, too, was a November Masters—the first time the tournament had ever been played outside March or April. That rendered the proceedings all the more bizarre, without the traditional azaleas in bloom and the grass in the rough (or "first cut," as the tournament refers to it) taller because it could not be cut with mowers as a result of not being rooted deeply enough given the time of year.

Without the 30,000 to 40,000 patrons on the grounds per day, the club opted not to put up ropes to line the fairways, tee boxes, and greens. That made for a very disorientating walk around the course to those accustomed to navigating the maze of ropes and crossing paths.

The lack of sound, too, was jarring; the silence, deafening.

"You're on the putting green up on [hole No.] 1 and you can hear eagles down on 13," Tiger Woods said before the tournament began. "That's what this tournament is all about, and we're not going to have that this year. It's going to be very different."

Woods spoke of how the vociferous support of the thousands of patrons in 2019 "helped me win" a fifth green jacket. "The support that I had, the energy that was around the property, it was electric that day," he recalled.

"The atmosphere, the crowds, the patrons, the feelings that you normally have here that you didn't quite have," Rory McIlroy said after he finished his final round.

"It's different," Tony Finau said. "The golf course is still amazing. But it just looks so different. I think the last time I played a competitive round here was in the final group with Tiger in '19. The difference between that and being out here in a practice round and getting ready is like night and day when it comes to how many people are around, the energy."

———

A Personal View

As one of the media members who was credentialed and fortunate enough to be on-site—after being COVID-19 tested before I was permitted onto the grounds (a requirement for everyone)—I had a few selfish moments when I soaked in the serenity of being able to walk around Augusta National unencumbered and in silence.

The first thing I did when I got to the course was march directly to Amen Corner, where the crowds usually take up the entire hill behind the 12th tee and pack the grandstand there. I stood 10 feet behind the 12th tee with no one in front of me and watched, for what felt like hours, players hitting their tee shots toward the green into that majestic and famous background over Rae's Creek.

Throughout the week, because there were no patrons and no grandstands to navigate around, I saw more shots up-close from places I'd never seen before in my 25 previous years covering the tournament.

Selfishly speaking, of course, there was a distinctively cool and unique element to it all. But I'd trade it in a heartbeat for the way it always has been and always should be—with the place filled with the patrons that create the unmistakable buzz and energy that electrify Augusta National during Masters week.

I walked away from the 2020 Masters hoping to never again have that front-row view behind the 12th tee or the sixth and 16th greens or on 18 or anywhere else on the grounds. I left hoping that the next Masters and every one after that was back to so-called normal, whatever that was going to end up being.

———

Different Conditions

The players felt the same way about the golf course, which yielded more birdies, eagles, and red numbers for sub-par rounds than usual because of the soft conditions created by the rye grass over-seed and the wet weather.

As Spain's Jon Rahm walked up the 18th fairway on Sunday with his final-round playing partner, 2018 Masters champion Patrick Reed, they talked about what the conditions might be like for the 2021 Masters, which would arrive in a mere five months.

"You almost have to hit the delete button from what you learned this week because it's never, ever going to play like this again," Rahm, who finished in a tie for seventh at 10-under par, said to Reed. "I hope they make it as firm as possible. The complete opposite of what we saw this week. I kind of hope we see the opposite and see a more challenging Masters."

———

Ghost Town

Outside the gates of Augusta National, it felt even more surreal than on the inside, knowing a Masters was taking place on the golf course but with none of the fanfare, the pomp and circumstance that usually surrounds the iconic event.

Washington Road, the honky-tonk four-lane highway off of which the entrance to Augusta National sits, a road dotted with strip malls and chain restaurants, was dead quiet. During Masters week, the traffic chokes Washington Road, overwhelming it, from the exit off of Interstate 20, past the club, and into downtown Augusta.

The usual exterior Masters trimmings that include the ticket brokers and scalpers skulking about on every street corner, private parties under temporary tents, and people selling whatever they can sell—highlighted by John Daly hawking his personalized souvenirs from his RV in front of Hooters—were all missing.

The restaurants at which you usually can't score a table to eat dinner during the seven days of Augusta's Masters week were half-empty. Mark Cumins, owner of TBonz Steakhouse, which has been nicknamed Augusta National's "unofficial 19th hole," peered around the goings-on at his restaurant on the Saturday night of Masters week, and when he was asked how business was going, he said, "About like a normal Saturday night in November."

That, of course, is not what businesses want during Masters week. Augusta businesses count on Masters week to at least double, triple, or quadruple their usual intake. Masters week has been called "Augusta's second Christmas" for the added revenue it generates for the city.

Broad Street, the main drag that runs through downtown Augusta, where restaurants and bars are teeming with customers during Masters week, looked like a ghost town, with smatterings of the few people in town patronizing them.

The palpable energy that engulfs Augusta and the surrounding area during Masters week was missing, and it was all a bit depressing. But at the same time, there were few people involved who weren't thankful that the 84th Masters took place at all considering the frightening state of the country and world at the time with the coronavirus still very much a threat.

————

MONDAY

Lee Elder Honored

Monday was a much quieter day than usual, not only because there were no patrons, but because much of the media had not yet arrived. But players quietly went about their business in practice rounds, spending countless hours on the practice grounds—not only to get ready, but what else was there to do but practice?

The powers that be at Augusta National used this quiet day to make a significant announcement: they were naming some local university scholarships that they fund for Lee Elder, who was the first black man to compete in a Masters, in 1975.

Masters chairman Fred Ridley, too, announced that Elder would join Jack Nicklaus and Gary Player as an Honorary Starter for the 2021 Masters, hitting a ceremonial tee shot off the first tee to begin that year's tournament.

Elder, 86 in 2020, received death threats in 1975 when he became the first black player invited to the Masters, qualifying after he won the 1974 Monsanto Open. He played in the Masters five times, with a career-best finish 17th place in 1979, and won four times on the PGA Tour and another eight times on the PGA Tour Champions.

Ridley said the club would be funding two golf scholarships at nearby Paine College, a historically black college, as well as funding the start-up of a women's golf program at the school.

"The courage and commitment of Lee Elder and other trailblazers like him inspired men and women of color to pursue their rightful opportunity to compete and follow their dreams," Ridley said. "But in reality, that opportunity is still elusive for many. We have a long way to go, and we can and we must do more. At Augusta National we believe in the power of the game of golf, to develop leaders, to spark progress, to provide opportunity, and to inspire dreams.

"Among the ways we exercise this belief is using our resources from the Masters Tournament to support our long-standing, unrestricted annual donation to Paine College, one of America's historically black colleges and universities located right down the street here in Augusta. We believe the time to do more is now. And Lee has graciously agreed to join our efforts as the namesake of the Lee Elder Scholarship."

Elder called the honor "heartwarming," adding, "It was a special moment for me. This will allow me to be a part of something much more than just hitting a ball off the first tee. It's something that I'll cherish for a lifetime.

"The opportunity to earn an invitation to the Masters and stand at that first tee was my dream and to have it come true in 1975 remains one of the greatest highlights of my career and life," he said. "So, to be invited back to the first tee one more time to join Jack and Gary for next year's Masters means the world to me."

The tournament's addition of Elder to the Honorary Starter group was special, but it felt overdue, with Elder never having been acknowledged enough for breaking the color barrier at Augusta National.

Augusta National has had its well-documented issues with race relations, dating back to its early years when the only men of color on the grounds were working in the kitchen or wearing white coveralls as caddies.

Asked if he's "satisfied" with the club's efforts to become more diverse, Ridley said, "I don't think 'satisfied' would be the right word. I would say that we do have a diverse membership. That has been an increasing fact over the past few years. It will continue to be an increasing fact during my chairmanship.

"I think what's important is that we continue to look at diversity always as we look at our membership," Ridley went on. "While progress can always and should be made, and we do have progress to be made, I can assure you that that is an issue that we're focused on."

Perhaps that Monday announcement was, in its own way, evidence of that.

When Elder was making history in 1975, he famously told reporters: "I belong."

Shortly after Ridley's announcement honoring Elder became public, Tiger Woods offered this endorsement via his Twitter account: "We all belong. Such wonderful news to hear from Augusta National in celebration of Lee Elder."

Better late than never.

———

TUESDAY

Birthday Hole-in-One

Jon Rahm had already had the thrill of acing the par-3 fourth hole in his practice round on Monday. And then this: he holed out on the par-3 16th hole while skipping his tee shot across the water of Rae's Creek.

Players skipping shots onto the 16th green has become one of the many cherished traditions at the Masters, because the skill wows the thousands of patrons lining the hole and watching from the grandstands behind the tee.

It's become a classic crowd-pleaser—to the point where the patrons are sometimes pleading with players to give it a go.

At this Masters, of course, there were no patrons to egg the players on. Still, some players tried their respective hands at it— even without the fanfare. Rahm was one of them and he holed out after his ball took a circuitous route, over the water, onto the green, and into the hole to the back-left pin location.

Oh yes, and it took place on his 26th birthday. The Masters has a way of providing magical moments like this—even in a pandemic.

"Pretty nice birthday present," Rahm said. "Can't complain. The second hole-in-one of the week. [Monday] on 4 I hit a 5 iron and we didn't know it went in. A couple people on the green, and we didn't know until we basically got to the green. Clearly we were all pretty shocked."

————

Champions Dinner Powers On

One of the traditions that did go on as scheduled during Masters week was the annual Champions Dinner at the clubhouse, where Tiger Woods hosted as the defending 2019 champion.

Woods, 44 at the time, went retro on the menu—which the defending champion traditionally chooses—going back to what he's served before: chicken and steak fajitas, along with sushi and milkshakes.

Because of the pandemic, the past champions were socially distanced at tables and seven former Masters champions were absent, the most since Ben Hogan created the Masters Club in 1952. So, of 33 possible attendees, 26 sat inside the first-floor Trophy Room, a change in venue from the customary second-floor library.

Among the missing past champions were 97-year-old Jackie Burke, Jr., who hasn't returned since 2011, Tom Watson, Raymond Floyd, Fuzzy Zoeller, Ian Woosnam, Ángel Cabrera, and Sergio García, who was forced to withdraw from the tournament because he'd tested positive for COVID-19 and had to quarantine.

Two-time winner Ben Crenshaw served as emcee of the dinner and he honored Hogan, reading aloud the letter Hogan wrote when he create the dinner in 1952, which read, in part: "Surely this has to be the most exclusive club of all. Not only do a fortunate few of us have the tournament to look forward to, but the annual meeting of our club as well. Here, long after serious competition for some of us comes to an end, we can still get together and reminisce."

Charles Coody, the 1971 winner, called the moment "emotional," adding, "I think it touched all of us."

No one was as emotional as Woods, who resurrected his fledgling career with that 2019 Masters victory, his first major championship in 11 years after a litany of health and personal issues had derailed his brilliant career.

"Tiger was very emotional," Jack Nicklaus said of Woods at the dinner. "I've never seen Tiger that way."

Gary Player recounted Woods revealing to those at the dinner that he had an emotional moment on his way to the club that evening.

"Tiger was really remarkable at the dinner this year as a host," Player said. "It was very heartwarming listening to him speak. He said he was on the way to the golf course and he had to stop because he had tears in his eyes and paused for a little while on the road because a lot of memories were going through his mind very quickly, to have won the tournament again with his children there. He paused for a while and he spoke very, very well."

Earlier in the day, in his pre-tournament press conference, Woods' voice cracked and his eyes got moist with tears when he recounted hugging his children alongside the 18th green after he won in 2019, a moment that was a flashback to him embracing his late father, Earl, in the same spot after he won his first Masters in 1997.

"I'm getting chills thinking about it," Woods said as he recounted the moment. "Coming up 18, and knowing that all I have to do is just two-putt that little 15-footer and to see my family there and my mom and my kids and all of the people that helped support me or were there for me in the tough times, and I was walking up there trying not to lose it, and still saying, 'Hey, I've still got to two-putt this.'

"Then I walked off the back of the green, to see [my son] Charlie there, just opened up our arms, it meant a lot to me and still does. It just reminded me so much of me and my dad, and to come full circle like that, it stills gets me, you know, a little teary.

"Pretty good bookends."

Woods also soaked in the gravity of getting to host the Champions Dinner for the fifth time.

"I may never have the opportunity to take the jacket off property again, so this means a lot to me," he said. "To have this opportunity to have the Champions Dinner and to be able to host it with all the guys that are here, it's going to be awfully special for me."

———

WEDNESDAY

What Will Bryson Do?

Wednesday was the first day one of the most popular Masters traditions was missing. The annual Par-3 Contest was not held in 2020 because of the pandemic and having no patrons and added player family members. It's usually the most popular spectator event of the week, drawing thousands of patrons around the iconic nine-hole gem.

As players went about their final preparations, there was a quiet concern amongst tournament officials on the eve of the opening round that some of the competitors might tear Augusta National apart because of the growing presence of length in the game combined with the fact that the golf course was extremely soft with wet conditions.

One player in particular, Bryson DeChambeau, was in the spotlight. Before the tournament began, DeChambeau spoke frankly about the fact that he was reaching the green on the 350-yard par-3 third hole with driver or 3-wood and he was hitting wedge into the par-5 13th hole.

DeChambeau fueled the hype around his length by saying he viewed Augusta National as a "par-67," not the par-72 it actually is.

"I'm looking at it as a par-67 for me because I can reach all the par-5s in two, no problem," DeChambeau said boldly. "If the conditions stay the way they are, that's what I feel like par is for me. That's not me being big-headed. I can hit it as far as I want to, but it comes down to putting and chipping out here. That is one of the things I think people sometimes struggle to see. As much as I can gain an advantage off the tee, I still have to putt it well and chip it well and wedge it well, and that's what I did at the U.S. Open."

DeChambeau, of course, annihilated the field in his six-shot U.S. Open victory two months earlier at Winged Foot, a golf course with much narrower fairways and deeper rough than Augusta National. Entering the 2020 Masters, there were people wondering aloud whether DeChambeau might "break" venerable Augusta National.

Gary Player offered what he called "a lovely little story about Bobby Jones" as it related to DeChambeau and his ungodly length.

"He was sitting next to me at the Champions [Locker] Room, and he was bent over and riddled with arthritis and he asked me to put the fork in his hand," Player recalled. "Then he said, 'Would you mind cutting my meat?' So, I cut his meat into little squares, and he ate it. I was always wanting to ask him a question. I said, 'Mr. Jones, may I ask you a question, sir?' He said, 'Certainly.' I said, 'You designed the golf course. I can never birdie the third hole.' And his reply was, 'You're not supposed to birdie the third hole.'

"And how he would be turning in his grave now to see Bryson DeChambeau say, 'Well, I'm taking a 3-wood just to put it in the middle of the green on the right.' Change is the price of survival, isn't it?"

DeChambeau entered the week leading the PGA Tour in driving distance with a 344.4-yard average.

"Every day, I'm trying to get faster and stronger and I'm trying to hit it as far as possible," DeChambeau said. "I have no idea where the end game is on this. I've only seen improvements in strength increase, I've obviously felt better every day, so I really don't know where the end game is on this.

"I am hitting it further now than I was at the U.S. Open. And I'm trying a driver this week that may help me hit it even a little bit further, so we'll see."

Indeed, DeChambeau was tinkering with a 48-inch driver during practice rounds, though he never put it in play.

"It's a substantially easier golf course for him than it is for everybody else," Justin Thomas said before the tournament began. "Once he starts messing with that longer driver and has a little bit more free time, then as crazy as it is, he might be able to hit it further. Pretty much every hole he's going to have a pretty distinct advantage over everybody."

Phil Mickelson called DeChambeau "a huge asset to the game of golf because we have a lot of people talking about what he's doing."

"He's thinking outside the box and he's willing to put in the work to accomplish it," Mickelson said. "I've had a chance to see how hard he works in other areas—whether it's brainwaves and his mental and cognitive function or what he eats. He works as hard as anybody does and thinks outside of the box in what is possible within the rules to create an advantage, and I have a lot of respect for that.

"I mean, the guy has made some massive changes that has required a lot of work and scrutiny, and he's putting himself out there and doing it. I hope it pays off for him at some point like it did at the U.S. Open. He's going to end up winning here at some point, whether it's this week or in the future. He's got the game and the brilliance, the work ethic, dedication."

Tiger Woods, who often plays practice rounds with DeChambeau, said, "What Bryson has done has been absolutely incredible, and we have all been amazed at what he's been able to do in such a short span of time. It's never been done before."

As DeChambeau and the rest of the world would find out as the 2020 Masters played out is that what appears to be a sure thing isn't always a sure thing. Not at the Masters. Not in sports. Not in life.

———

THURSDAY

Honorary Starters Tee Off

Another of the annual traditions the club carried out in 2020 was the Honorary Starters kicking the tournament off with ceremonial tee shots first thing in the morning Thursday.

As has been the case most recently, Jack Nicklaus and Gary Player did the honors, and they did so in a dank, chilly mist Thursday morning that included a two-and-a-half-hour rain delay.

The highlight of this edition was Nicklaus "employing" his wife, Barbara, as his caddie, clad in the traditional white caddie coveralls.

Nicklaus has five children and 22 grandchildren and usually rotates caddie duties among them. But because of the protocols allowing players and members to have only one guest, there were no Nicklaus kids or grandkids at Augusta in 2020.

"Normally I have one of the grandkids, and of course we couldn't bring anybody except our spouses this time," he said. "Last night I said to her, 'I think it would be kind of fun if you would put on a caddie uniform and do that,' and she said, 'Oh, I don't want to do that.' I said, 'Yeah, you do, it'll be fun.'"

She did it and Nicklaus hit his tee shot into the first fairway.

"I was pleased that it was dark because you couldn't see where my ball went," Nicklaus joked.

There will be a time when the legends from yesteryear like Nicklaus and Player will no longer be around, so the question was posed to both Woods and Phil Mickelson, the two best players of the current generation, what they thought about being a part of that ceremony down the road.

"Thirty years from now? That's a long time," Woods joked. "The fact that I had an opportunity to watch Byron Nelson and Sam Snead tee off there, and to see even Jack and Arnold [Palmer] and Gary, and now to have Lee start next year, whether it's Phil and I down the road or whatever it may be, it's up to the chairman, and it's an honor [to] start off the Masters."

Woods then joked of Mickelson, who's always been obsessed with distance: "Hopefully that will be us one day, and I'll be hitting bombs past him."

"Well, he's only 44…and he's going to be competing and hopefully playing in these events and being in contention for a number of years [and] I'm going to try to be with him," Mickelson, who's five years older than Woods, countered. "That's really not on our radar right now. If that was something we got asked to do that would be really cool. That's really a special thing."

———

Bryson's Rough Start

Once the ceremonial tee shots were struck, the 2020 tournament began and all eyes were on DeChambeau, who had a morning tee time in the opening round. It didn't go well.

He ended up shooting a 2-under-par 70, but it was sloppy, lowlighted by a messy double bogey he took on the par-5 13th, one of the holes tournament officials feared he'd make a mockery of. Instead, the 13th made a mockery of DeChambeau, who took a double-bogey 7 on it.

It began with a 324-yard drive through the right side of the fairway and into the trees. Faced with a 194-yard shot off pine straw, through two pine trees, and over the tributary that feeds Rae's Creek, DeChambeau pull-hooked his second shot, sending the ball well left of the green and into the shrubbery.

After hitting a provisional ball that ended up in the water, DeChambeau found his first ball in the bushes, took an unplayable lie, and duffed his next shot. He pitched onto the green with his fifth shot to within 12 feet of the hole and two-putted for double bogey.

That left DeChambeau, who began his round on No. 10, at 2-over par through his first four holes.

By the time his round was over, DeChambeau was 2-under par for the day, tied with 62-year-old Larry Mize, who averaged 247 yards off the tee.

"This golf course, as much as I'm trying to attack it, it can bite back," a humbled DeChambeau said after his round. "It's still Augusta National, and it's the Masters. It's an amazing test of golf no matter what way you play it. I tried to take on some risk today. It didn't work out as well as I thought it would have, but at the end of the day I'm proud of the way I handled myself and finished off—birdieing 8 and 9 was a testament to my focus level, and wanting to contend here."

———

Casey Takes Early Lead

While all eyes were on DeChambeau, the opening round belonged to Paul Casey, a 43-year-old Englishman who, in the previous Masters, opened with a 9-over-par 79 en route to missing the cut.

Casey carded a 7-under-par 65 to take the first-round lead.

By the time the first day ended, 50 of the 92 players in the field were under par, including those still in the midst of their opening round to be completed Friday because of the weather delay. Thirty-three players were 2-under or better.

Casey, with his 16-shot swing from the first round of the 2019 Masters to 2020, unofficially won the "most improved" award, which came with no trophy or crystal.

Asked what, other than 16 shots, was different about this opening round and the one in 2019, Casey said, "I have no idea. Just rubbish. I played some decent golf in 2019 overall, just not the first round of the Masters. I don't know why it was rubbish. I'm not blaming anybody. I take full responsibility. It was rubbish."

Because of the Thursday weather delay, 44 of the 92 players in the field were forced to complete their respective opening rounds on Friday morning.

———

FRIDAY

A Catch-Up Day

Friday was a catch-up day combining the conclusion of the rain-delayed first round and most of the second round.

By day's end, a fascinating weekend was set in place, with some of the game's biggest names littering the leaderboard.

Dustin Johnson, the No. 1 ranked player in the world, was tied for the lead with Justin Thomas, ranked No. 3, along with up-and-comers Abraham Ancer and Cam Smith—all of whom were 9-under par after Friday's second round.

Former Masters champion Danny Willet, who'd been in the wilderness since his 2016 victory, was 7-under, along with European Ryder Cup heroes Tommy Fleetwood and Justin Rose.

Even defending champion Tiger Woods was in touching distance of the lead, as was Phil Mickelson, who was 5-under par through 36 holes, four shots behind the leaders.

"I'm striking the ball exceptional, and I'm putting horrific," Mickelson said after his Friday round.

Mickelson, who at 50 had won the two 2020 Champions Tour events, was bullish on how long he was still hitting the ball with the driver, saying, "I'm driving like a stallion."

His run would be short-lived, as Mickelson faded on the weekend.

―――――

Lost Ball Mess

DeChambeau's lost week continued on Friday, and ironically the low point of the day came on that short par-3 third hole he bragged he'd been driving during practice rounds.

His tee shot missed the fairway left and seemingly plugged in the soggy rough. No one could find the ball, and DeChambeau was forced to go back and re-tee.

DeChambeau was understandably agitated. Marshals are on the grounds for the purpose of spotting errant shots in the rough or woods. But with the COVID-19 restrictions, there did not appear to be as many marshals working and, of course, there are no patrons allowed. So that reduced the number of eyes on DeChambeau's tee shot.

The debacle ended in a triple-bogey 7, fittingly on Friday the 13th of November. So, to review, DeChambeau took a total of 14 shots on No. 13 in the first round and No. 3 in the second round on holes he figured he'd take seven shots combined at worst.

Adding insult to injury: someone found DeChambeau's lost ball after the rules-allowed, three-minute window had expired and gave it to DeChambeau on the fourth tee.

"It definitely throws you for a loop when the guy goes and gives you the ball on the fourth tee box, like, 'Oh, I found it,'" DeChambeau said.

Louis Oosthuizen, one of DeChambeau's paying partners the first two rounds, said, "I could see he wasn't on his game, and you get those things. You get those days."

DeChambeau, the unanimous favorite to win the 2020 Masters at the start of the week, went on to bogey his next two holes and ended up making the cut on the number.

―――――

Langer Makes Masters History

Two-time Masters winner Bernhard Langer apparently thought this Masters was a Champions Tour event. The forever-young 63-year-old German who has dominated the senior circuit like no other player in history entered the weekend 3-under par and just six shots out of the lead in his 37th Masters. Langer making the cut overtook Tommy Aaron as the oldest player ever to do so.

When informed that he was the oldest player to make the Masters cut, Langer said, "How about that? I'll drink to that."

Asked what he was drinking, he said, "Shandy."

"There have been so many great players here before me, including Jack Nicklaus to Gary Player to all the greats that have competed here, and to be the oldest to make the cut, it's certainly an achievement," Langer said. "Hopefully, I get to play a few more years and enjoy this place."

More on Langer and his remarkable story later.

―――――

Rory Slam Bid Fizzles

Rory McIlroy, in his sixth try to complete the career Grand Slam, a feat only five other players have ever accomplished, walked off the golf course Friday regretting how he'd played Thursday and wondering what might have been.

McIlroy, who needs only a Masters victory to become the sixth player ever to win all four major championships, shot 75 in the opening round, which he completed on the Friday of the tournament.

McIlroy rallied to shoot a 6-under-par 66 in his second round Friday—a nine-shot swing.

After the sloppy first 18, he wondered afterward, "Where the hell did that come from?"

"I knew it was in there, it was just a matter of trusting a little more and being committed," he said.

SATURDAY

DJ Takes Charge

He'd been quietly lurking all week, playing consistent and great golf. And by day's end Saturday, Dustin Johnson had opened a four-shot lead entering the final round.

Earlier in the week, Johnson was asked what his favorite Masters tradition is.

"The sandwiches," he responded.

Asked which one, he responded, "All of them."

That opinion was sure to change on Sunday as he marched toward his second career major championship, doing it in record-shattering fashion. Johnson's third-round 65 got him to 16-under par, within two shots of the tournament record of 18-under, shared by Tiger Woods and Jordan Spieth.

Johnson led Sungjae Im (68 in the third round), Abraham Ancer (69), and Cam Smith (69)—all of whom were 12-under par—by four shots.

Johnson was ranked No. 1 in the world and was the game's hottest player. In his six previous tournaments, he'd finished runner-up, won, finished runner-up, won, finished sixth, and finished runner-up.

Despite the large lead, however, Johnson slipping on the green jacket was hardly *fait accompli* based on his checkered history with 54-hole leads. In his career entering that final round, Johnson had converted only 10-of-22 PGA Tour leads into victories. In majors, he was 0-for-4, having lost the PGA Championship that August at Harding Park to Collin Morikawa, along with the 2010, 2015, and 2018 U.S. Opens.

"If I can play like I did [Saturday], I think it will break that streak," Johnson said that Saturday evening. "I put myself in the situation a lot of times. I know what it takes. I know how I respond in this situation. I'm very comfortable with having the lead going into [Sunday]. I've been in this situation a lot of times. I'm looking forward to the challenge. The game is in really good form right now."

Johnson said his form felt "very similar to what it was back in 2017," when he was the favorite to win the Masters but never made it to the first tee due to a fall at the home he was renting, injuring his lower back and forcing him to withdraw before the first round.

"I'm going to have to go out and play well if I'm going to put that green jacket on [Sunday]," Johnson said on Saturday.

"If DJ goes out there and plays really solid like [Saturday], it's going to be pretty much impossible to catch him," Ancer said.

Incredibly, Johnson was only five weeks removed from testing positive for COVID-19. His first tournament back after quarantining was the week before the Masters, in Houston, where he finished runner-up.

———

Rory Wows Langer

While Johnson was positioning himself for victory on Saturday, McIlroy was paired with Bernhard Langer in the third round, and it was compelling theater.

McIlroy was a 31-year-old in his prime; Langer was 63 and the oldest player ever to make the cut at the Masters.

McIlroy had what Langer wishes he still had: length.

But, of more importance, Langer had what McIlroy wants more than anything in his professional life: a green jacket.

Langer won the Masters in 1985 and 1993 and has a spot of his own in the Champions Locker Room, where his green jacket hangs. He, too, has an invite to the tournament every year for the rest of his life, a place-setting at the annual Champions Dinner.

McIlroy, after the opening-round 75 that sabotaged him, followed his second-round 66 with a third-round 67. But he was too far behind Johnson to even entertain the thought of winning.

He conceded that he'll "look back at [the first round] and rue some of the shots that I hit and some of the thought processes I had and just try to learn from it and be better the next time."

"The good golf was in there; I just didn't allow myself to play that way on the first 18 holes," he went on. "This course can do that. This course can make you a little bit careful and a little bit tentative at times. I've always said I play my best golf when I'm trusting and freer, and I've been a lot freer over the last 36 holes."

Langer's tee shots seemed miles behind McIlroy's all day.

"I don't think the course has ever played this long," Langer said. "I don't remember hitting 3-woods into so many par-4s…and hybrids. I mean, on 17, I hit a beautiful drive and I hit 2-hybrid. Rory hit driver and pitching wedge. That's what I'm competing against."

Langer estimated that McIlroy's tee shots were "some 40, sometimes 80 or 100" yards beyond his.

When those numbers were relayed to McIlroy, he joked, "I'd like to know where the 40 was."

Turning serious, McIlroy marveled at the ageless Langer.

"I try to think about what scores I would shoot if I was hitting it where he hit it," McIlroy said. "Honestly, it's like me playing an 8,500-yard golf course. That's what it's like. It's so impressive, just the way he methodically plots his way around and gets it up and down when he needs to. It's really cool to watch. I wish in 30 years' time I'm back here doing the exact same thing."

———

SUNDAY

The Final Round

Sunday was always going to be about Dustin Johnson. This was his Masters from the start of the week, and he finished it in brilliant style.

Much was different about this Masters.

The month it was played, delayed from April to November because of COVID-19.

The eerie silence with no patrons permitted on the grounds because of concerns of spreading the virus, leaving the tournament without its signature roars, particularly in the cauldron of the back nine with players making runs.

And then there was the winner, Johnson, closing out a 54-hole lead in a major championship for the first time in his career after previously going 0-for-4 in majors entering the final round with a lead.

Johnson, 36, was brilliant after a shaky start to the day, shooting a final-round 4-under-par 68 to finish at 20-under par for the tournament, breaking the Masters record of 18-under par held by Tiger Woods in 1997 and Jordan Spieth in 2015.

He won his second career major by five shots, the largest margin at the Masters since Woods won by 12 in 1997.

Cam Smith from Australia and Sungjae Im from Korea finished tied for second at 15-under par, but neither ever truly challenged Johnson, who methodically plotted his way to victory.

For the week, Johnson carded only four bogeys in 72 holes, setting another Masters record, beating out Nicklaus and Jimmy Demaret, both of whom had five. He missed only 12 greens all week, a record last set by defending-champion Woods.

When Johnson's four-shot lead evaporated to a mere stroke through five holes, his issues closing out 54-hole leads in majors crept into people's minds. But Johnson regained control when he stuffed a tee shot to six feet on the par-3 sixth hole, made the birdie putt, and never looked back.

"I'm sure a lot of you all think...there were doubts in my mind, just because I had been there," Johnson said. "I'm in this position a lot of times. When am I going to have the lead and finishing off a major? It definitely proved that I can do it."

He did it in style, capturing his 24th PGA Tour career victory, a number bettered by only Woods (82) and Mickelson (44) among active players.

Johnson became the first No. 1–ranked player in the world to win the Masters since Woods did it in 2002. The win was his fourth of 2020, including the Tour Championship, which gave him the PGA Tour's FedEx Cup title. Since the beginning of 2015, Johnson has won 15 times worldwide, including the 2016 U.S. Open.

————

Langer Gets Another Dose of Distance

Before Dustin Johnson put the finishing touches on his victory, as usual, there were some compelling stories from outside of the final pairing around Augusta National that unfolded on Sunday.

For all the contrasting fascination of Rory McIlroy and Bernhard Langer paired together on Saturday, Langer played with Bryson DeChambeau in Sunday's final round, afterward conceding that he watched McIlroy and DeChambeau "in awe."

"Every once in awhile I had to tell myself, 'Stop watching and play your game. Focus on what you want to do,'" Langer said. "I got to experience the longest guys in the world right now, and it's quite amazing."

In the final round, Langer shot 71 to DeChambeau's 73.

"Even though I'm bombing it by him, he's still playing better than me," DeChambeau said. "That's the cool part about the game of golf. You can shoot a score whatever way you want, and he's able to do it still at his age."

————

Bryson's Flameout

The postscript to DeChambeau's 2020 Masters was a sobering one. He revealed earlier in the tournament that he was not feeling well physically, so badly that he went for a COVID-19 test (which came back negative) on Friday evening.

"I've got to fix whatever is going on up here," DeChambeau said. "I [felt] dizziness. At the beginning of the week I felt like I could have a great chance to win the tournament if I just played my game. I made way too many mistakes.

"It just seems like there's a lot of things going not the right way," DeChambeau surmised. "I've certainly played worse golf than this and won golf tournaments. It's golf. You can't control everything as much as you try."

Two problems here:

DeChambeau is the classic control freak and when he's unable to control his environment, he struggles.

He also brought too many distractions with him to Augusta, beginning with the plan to test out that 48-inch driver during practice rounds. There's an adage in pro golf: never go to a major championship trying to find your game. DeChambeau did just that in the 2020 Masters and it cost him dearly.

————

Tiger's 10 on 12

A shocking lowlight to the Sunday final round was the 10 Tiger Woods carded on the par-3 12th hole, where he hit three balls into Rae's Creek.

It was the highest score Woods has even taken on a hole in his PGA Tour career. His previous high was nine at the 1997 Memorial, on the par-4 third hole in the third round.

Incredibly, the 10 wasn't the worst score on No. 12's history. Tom Weiskopf posted a 13 on No. 12 in 1980.

In the most stunning irony of all, Woods very much won last year's Masters on the 12th hole when his closest competitors Francesco Molinari, Tony Finau, and Brooks Koepka all hit their tee shots into the water while Woods seized control of the tournament.

"I committed to the wrong wind," Woods explained. "The wind was off the right for the first two guys, and then when I stepped up there, it switched to howling off the left. I didn't commit to the wind, and I also got ahead of it and pushed it, too, because I thought the wind would come more off the right and it was off the left, and that just started the problem from there.

"From there, I hit a lot more shots and had a lot more experiences there in Rae's Creek. This is unlike any other sport in which you're so alone out there and you have to figure it out…and I did coming in."

Indeed, after the 10 on 12, Woods birdied five of the final six holes to scratch out a final-round 76 to finish the week 1-under par.

"I've hit a few too many shots than I wanted to today, and I will not have the chairman be putting the green jacket on me; I'll be passing it on," Woods joked.

On the 12th, Woods hit 8-iron from 155 yards that hit on the front of the green and rolled back into the creek. Then, he dropped in front of the creek with 70 yards to the pin, and again spun the ball into the water.

Dropping again and taking a second penalty stroke, Woods went long with his fifth shot into the back-right bunker. From there, he hit a thin wedge out of the sand and the ball skidded across the green and back into the water.

After dropping for his seventh shot, he played his eighth again from the bunker, got the shot onto the green, and two-putted for the 10.

Woods called the mess on the 12th hole "part of our sport."

"This sport is awfully lonely sometimes," he said. "You have to fight it. No one is going to bring you off the [pitcher's] mound or call in a sub. You have to fight through it. That's what makes this game so unique and so difficult mentally.

"We've all been there, unfortunately. Unfortunately, I've been there and you just have to turn around and figure out the next shot, and I was able to do that coming home."

Too little, of course, too late.

————

The Winner

Woods, of course, hung around so he could participate in the Masters tradition of the defending champion awarding the green jacket to the winner.

When the tournament was over and Woods had slipped the green jacket over Johnson's shoulders at the winner's ceremony, Woods even became emotional watching Johnson show rare emotion.

The scene at the 18th hole was an incredible contrast to what took place in April of 2019, when Woods won his fifth green jacket and thousands of fans chanted his name when he walked off the green to the clubhouse.

When Johnson walked off 18, a number of fellow players were there to congratulate him, including Masters champions Bubba Watson, Zach Johnson, and Jordan Spieth, all of whom were wearing their green jackets, along with Justin Thomas and Rickie Fowler.

When Johnson spotted Watson, he told him: "I've been dreaming of putting that jacket on my whole life."

Johnson grew up about an hour away from Augusta, in Irmo, South Carolina, and never played Augusta National until he qualified to play in his first Masters, in 2009.

"Growing up so close to here, it's always been a tournament I wanted to win the most," Johnson said. "Being close the last couple years, finishing second last year to Tiger, this one was just something that I really wanted to do. [Even] starting today with a four-shot lead, I knew it wasn't going to be easy. It was still hard. I was nervous all day, but I felt like I controlled myself very well."

A classic Dustin Johnson moment: as he walked up the 18th fairway with a five-shot lead, he asked Austin, "Where do I stand?"

Asked afterward if he honestly didn't know, Johnson said, "I did not. Not exactly. I mean, I assumed I had the lead, but I didn't know by how many. That was kind of my goal. I kind of looked at the leaderboard a little bit early, and after that I told myself, 'Don't worry about what anybody's doing. Just play as good as you can.'"

It was more than enough.

Entering that week, Johnson had done about everything you can do at Augusta National without winning a Masters. In his previous four starts, he finished runner-up in 2019, tied for 10th in 2018, tied for fourth in 2016, and tied for sixth in 2015 (missing 2017 with an injury).

"He's been knocking on the door so long, and since coming back in June [after] the lockdown, he has been by far the best player in the world," Rory McIlroy said. "He's won a few times, won the [2020] FedEx Cup, had a chance at Harding Park [at the 2020 PGA]. I think it validates what he did at Oakmont a few years ago [winning the 2016 U.S. Open] and he's had so many chances and hasn't quite been able to close the deal, but his resume speaks for itself—how many times he's won on the PGA Tour, how consistent he's been.

"I played with him the first two days here. He's got the ball on a string. It was really impressive."

———

Changing Impressions

Johnson's victory—and the way he reacted to it—changed many people's impressions of him as a robotic, aloof, passionless player.

Johnson has been viewed by so many as a player so detached that nothing affects him, win or lose, that he cares so little the wins are ho-hum and the losses don't bother him, that he's so talented he's never really had to work very hard and he has no emotions.

The green jacket winner's ceremony on the practice green after his victory changed all of that.

As cool, calm, collected, and borderline catatonic as he appeared on the golf course, dusting his nearest competitors by five shots and posting a tournament-record 20-under par, Johnson was an emotional mess while being awarded the green jacket.

With the practice green ringed with about 400 people, consisting of tournament officials, Augusta members, player families, and media, Johnson was being interviewed by CBS TV's Amanda Balionis and he cried.

Yes, Dustin Johnson cried.

He had to pause several times to compose himself as he tried to answer Balionis' questions.

"It's a dream come true…as a kid I always dreamed of being a Masters champion," Johnson said.

He looked over at his longtime girlfriend and mother of his children, Paulina Gretzky; his brother and caddie, Austin; his coach, Claude Harmon III; and some other members of his team—and Johnson froze. He couldn't speak.

"I'm sorry," Johnson said, pausing again. "I can't even talk. I've never had this much trouble gathering myself."

The players who spent the day chasing Johnson in vain only wish he had that much trouble making birdies and pars.

This may sound like sacrilege, but watching the way Johnson reacted to having the green jacket slipped over his shoulders by Tiger Woods on that practice green ceremony was more compelling theater than watching him win it.

When the CBS interview was over and as the gathering around the putting green dispersed, one of the Augusta National members clad in his green jacket was overhead to say to another, "They're all human."

That's the thing about Johnson. Outside of those who are closest to him, human is the last thing most of us viewed him as. Because he's so ridiculously talented and because the vibe he gives off screams indifference.

"He doesn't throw clubs or curse at me or do any of that stuff, and that's just because he's a class act," Austin Johnson said afterward. "That doesn't mean he doesn't care. The guy cares more than anybody. I think just because we're Southern guys, laid-back and talk a little slow, everybody thinks we don't really care."

Dustin Johnson said, "It means so much to me…it means so much to my family, Paulina, the kids. They know it's something that I've always been dreaming about and it's why I work so hard. To finally have the dream come true, I think that's why you see all that emotion."

All these years into a fantastic career, and it took a Masters victory to open our eyes to who Dustin Johnson really is.

———

Brother and Caddie a Key

It's funny: when Dustin Johnson hired Austin to caddie for him in 2013, there was a lot of eye-rolling amongst those around the game. Some joked about the pairing, calling them "Dumb and

Dumber," and criticized Johnson's decision to have his brother on his bag rather than a professional caddie.

But the two have become a formidable pair, with Austin having grown into the job and become a proficient reader of greens to aid his brother.

"When I started, I was more of a buddy, someone for him to hang out with," Austin said. "I'm a decent player. I know the game. But being a top caddie? Not even close. But I was a sponge. If I got close to [Jim] Bones Mackay [Phil Mickelson's former longtime caddie], I wouldn't leave his side. I'd ask him everything I could. Same with John Wood [another longtime caddie]. At these team events. I just learned. And I earned [Dustin's] trust. And it's gotten to where now he's leaned on me pretty heavily out there. I'm just glad it has worked out the way it has."

The Johnson brothers grew up an hour away from the gates to Augusta National. They hit balls well past darkness at a place called Weed Hill Driving Range in South Carolina, and every putt they rolled on the practice green was to win the imaginary Masters.

"They had lights on the range, and most nights I would shut the lights off when I was leaving," Dustin recalled.

Now, all these years later, the brothers were together on the 18th green at Augusta National. Dustin had just tapped in for par and the win and went straight over to his brother and hugged him, Austin wiping away tears.

"Yeah, I was trying to hold them back, but it was tough," Austin said. "This was the one we dreamed about growing up just down the road. I remember being out on the putting green late at night and every putt was to win the Masters."

Dustin called it "unbelievable having my brother on my bag," adding, "I just love experiencing all these moments with him. I wouldn't want it any other way."

Asked what Dustin was like Sunday morning with a four-shot lead entering the final round, Austin said, "He's always pretty much the same DJ—laid-back, pretty calm. You can't tell if we're coming down the stretch of a major or if we're laying on the couch watching football by his reactions.

"He seemed really focused this morning. He had his mind set on what he wanted to do and it didn't seem like anything was going to knock him off course from doing that."

Nothing did.

Since Dustin made Austin full-time caddie, the pair has 17 tournaments, including two major championships.

"I couldn't be more excited for him," Austin said. "I see how hard he works, and to be so close in a couple majors and come up just short. We got the one at Oakmont [the U.S. Open], but I think we've had four 54-hole leads and this was the first one we converted. It's a big weight off the shoulders for sure."

Austin said the near-misses "definitely hurt, but you learn a lot from those losses and I think we've implemented that. I think we've matured as a team and learned from not converting the leads and our mistakes."

Dustin's coach, Claude Harmon III, marveled at the formidable team the brothers have become.

"I think that the job that two of them have done, the team that the two of them have become this year has just been phenomenal," Harmon said. "It's been easy for everybody to look at the way DJ plays and just go, 'Well, you know, anybody can caddie for DJ.' If you talk to the caddies out here on tour, they all say that Austin has done a good job.

"If you look at what they've done on the greens, they've started to get into that routine every single time, and I think that's been huge for their confidence. I think the work that those two have done, it's just been amazing."

Dumb and Dumber. Who's laughing now?

————

Coach's High Praise

The way Claude Harmon III sees it, if a scientist in a lab was to construct the perfect golfer…that golfer would be Dustin Johnson.

Harmon, of course, is biased, because he's Johnson's swing coach. But he has a point about the 2020 Masters champion.

"If you could design a golfer, you'd design Dustin," Harmon said. "He's the living embodiment of everything every golf sports psychologist tells you—to stay in the present, have no memory. He's a freak athlete. Other than Jack [Nicklaus] and Tiger, he has one the greatest golf minds in history. He's a hell of a golfer. He doesn't get enough credit for being the golfer that he is."

That last statement is true and incredible considering the depth of Johnson's resume. His 24 career PGA Tour victories are superseded among active players only by Woods' 82 and Phil Mickelson's 44.

Johnson, too, has won at least one tournament in each of his 14 years on the PGA Tour, 15 of his 24 wins coming since 2016.

It's weird, though: before he so impressively staved off the field to win his second major championship on Sunday, the narrative of Johnson's career skewed far closer to the calamity and failure portion of it than the prolific winner part.

Johnson's brain freeze at the 2010 PGA Championship at Whistling Straits, where he grounded his club in what he thought was a waste area, but what tournament officials told every player in the field that week was a sand trap, cost him a major.

So, too, did the final-round 80 he shot at the 2010 U.S. Open at Pebble Beach that melted away the three-shot lead he took into the day.

Then there was the three-putt from 12 feet on the 72nd hole of the 2015 U.S. Open at Chambers Bay, handing the tournament to Jordan Spieth. A one-putt would have won and a two-putt would have sent them to a playoff.

Even when Johnson won his first major championship, the 2016 U.S. Open at Oakmont, that final round was marred with calamity, with USGA officials mulling whether his ball moved on a slick green after he'd addressed it (a two-shot penalty back then before the archaic rule was changed).

There were other incidents, too, like Johnson slicing his 2-iron out of bounds on the 14th hole of the 2011 British Open at Royal St. Georges, where he was in contention, trailing by two shots.

Some of these incidents, coupled with Johnson's flat-line, aloof demeanor, led people who don't know him to question his intelligence.

"He's smarter than you think," Rory McIlroy said.

How so?

"He's switched on—more so than he lets on, I'll just put it that way," McIlroy said.

Perhaps Johnson's most impressive trait—more than his amazing length off the tee, his beautifully rhythmic swing, underrated short game, and great putting—is his mind and the ability to shake off the disappointments and carry on to the next thing as if nothing happened to him.

"I think he's got one of the best attitudes in the history of the game," McIlroy said. "He makes the game so simple, or makes it look so simple at times."

It's because Johnson makes the game look so easy that he gives some people the impression that he lacks passion for the game, for winning.

"The misconception about Dustin is that things don't bother him," Harmon said. "But he just doesn't have any want or need to look back, because he knows that he can't really change anything that's happened in the past and he can't affect anything that happens in the future.

"When he missed that putt on 18 at Chambers Bay and was walking off the green in '15 and I would have told you everything that would happen from that point on…would you have believed it?" Harmon went on. "The scars were supposed to be too deep. He was never going to come back from that. But look at the run he's been on this year. Every single week he has a chance to win—second here [at Augusta] last year, second at the PGA [in August], sixth at the U.S. Open [in September]. That's the type of stuff that Jack and Tiger did."

Harmon called the 2020 Masters "an opportunity for him to flip the script and change the narrative" for Johnson.

"I think the narrative now looks very different than it did [Saturday] night—after being 0-for-4 with 54-hole leads [in majors] and all the things he's done," Harmon said.

Johnson's journey to changing that narrative has had its bumps in the road. People who worked closely with Johnson became frustrated because they felt he was wasting his talent by not caring or working enough. It was no secret on the PGA Tour that Johnson was a partier off the course.

Butch Harmon, who was Johnson's swing coach in the early 2010s, once said, "He has always relied on tremendous natural ability to carry him through. It's taken him all the way to being a top-10 player. But every other guy in the top 10 outworks him."

Joe LaCava, one of the most respected caddies in the game, worked for Johnson in 2011 before leaving him to work for Woods in 2011. The move raised eyebrows, because Johnson was a human ATM for a caddie and Woods was struggling to come back from injuries and scandal. But LaCava was quietly frustrated by Johnson's lack of commitment.

Johnson took a six-month "leave of absence" in 2014 to address "personal challenges," which was later reported by Golf.com to be an unannounced suspension by the PGA Tour for failing three drug tests, for both cocaine and marijuana.

Those times seem to long ago now when you look at Johnson's place in the game. By many accounts, Johnson completely changed his lifestyle and became doggedly committed to being the best.

Woods, who's had his share of off-the-course issues to overcome, was moved to tears as he listened to Johnson's emotional interview during the green jacket ceremony.

"As we've all seen, he's an amazing athlete," Woods said. "He's one of first guys to ever bring athleticism to our sport. DJ has such am amazing ability to stay calm in tough moments. And, in order to win this event—and we all know as past champions how hard it is with the emotions we have to deal with out there—there's no one more suited to that, I think, than DJ."

AUTHOR'S NOTE

The day after the Masters has been played, once the green jacket has been awarded, there's a one-day tournament on Augusta National that isn't televised and that few people know about.

On the Saturday of the third round, 28 members from the media are selected—via a lottery system—to play Augusta National on the Monday after the tournament has been decided.

The experience is not unlike what it must feel like for a non-professional athlete to take batting practice at Yankee Stadium or play a couple sets of tennis on Centre Court at Wimbledon.

The pins are in the same places they were for the final round. Everything is the same as the final round except for the empty grandstands, and the media play from the members tees, not the championship tournament tees.

If you're lucky enough to be selected, you are given a small blue ticket stub with a number on it that looks like one of those coat check tickets you're given at a restaurant, and you are not permitted to enter your name back into the lottery for the following seven years.

It took me five years of covering the Masters before I was selected. It was 1998, the year Mark O'Meara won the green jacket with a 20-foot birdie putt on 18 sealing it, and it was an experience that was as euphoric as it was harrowing.

Here's how it went:

It was 7:15 in the morning Monday, and I felt like the luckiest person on the face of the earth at that very moment, because I was standing on the first tee at Augusta National with a driver in my hands.

I was the everyday, accidental-tourist hacker whom the powers that be in green jackets normally don't allow to roam their course. But my ping-pong ball came up in the annual Masters media lottery.

I came to Augusta National committing a cardinal sin: I came without my swing, which sometime in the previous two weeks had gone from somewhat dependable to shank city.

Battling the onset of the dreaded shanks before a dream round like this is worse than having a couple nasty cold sores pop up around your mouth the morning of your wedding.

But I played the course anyway, because it felt like a once-in-a-lifetime dream come true, the ultimate round of golf.

At that time, the driving range was not open to the Monday interlopers, so there was no time to practice before the most important round of my life, no chance to try to work my way out of the shanks. Club officials have since modified the day-after experience, allowing the players to be "members for a day," driving down Magnolia Lane, using the Champions Locker Room and the practice facility.

So at that time, without as much as a practice swing on that early Augusta morning with the sun rising and the dew evaporating, I striped my first drive over the corner of the right fairway bunker. I'd never felt so euphoric. It was as if I was skydiving for the first time. My playing partner said to me, "Is this really happening? Are we really here?"

The entire experience is surreal, something I wish every person with an enthusiasm for the game could be a part of just once.

Walking up that first fairway, my tracks straight up the hill were the first of the day, like a skier carving the first turns into fresh powder. I had chills. For years I'd watched the greatest golfers in the world walk this very route.

Now I was inside the ropes.

I was Tiger Woods without the entourage, without the zillion-dollar endorsement deals, and without talent.

Then it all went awry. My euphoria morphed into horror when I realized I simply could not get an iron airborne.

After my perfect drive on No. 1 that left me with 128 yards to the green in perfect condition, I warned my caddie, "You're going to see some unorthodox things today," referring to advice I once got from a local New York pro to hit balls with my heels together to get rid of the shanks. So, as ridiculous as it looks, that's the way I played.

I proceeded to click my heels together like Dorothy from *The Wizard of Oz* and cold topped an 8-iron underneath the trees to the right of the green and was so afraid of hitting another iron, I used my putter to punch out from the trees—something I guarantee no pro did during that Masters week.

I somehow managed a 49 on the front nine, and then, shortly after the turn, the round—and my fragile psyche—would unravel.

My anticipated foray into Amen Corner was a wildly disappointing ride, despite how awestruck I was by the magnitude of it all.

My waltz through Amen Corner, which went double bogey, triple bogey, triple bogey on Nos. 11, 12, and 13, was the most pathetic performance on that hallowed ground since Greg Norman sputtered around this legendary corner two years prior en route to famously leaking away his six-stroke lead to hand the green jacket away to Nick Faldo.

I hit a fat 8-iron approach shot into the water on 11, though after a drop I hit a crisp sand wedge to eight feet and holed the putt to save double bogey.

The most humiliating moment came on No. 12, the famous par-3 at Amen Corner.

There was a backup at the 12th, the favorite photo-op place for players, and when my turn finally came to hit, I could feel those people on the tee looking at me and thinking, "What is this imbecile doing with his heels together?" Those were my thoughts in mid-backswing. I shanked a six-iron so far right it landed in the 13th fairway. I wanted to slink into the woods and disappear.

I'd been holding the round together with duct tape and Band-Aids, but now the dam had cracked. I somehow got a pitching wedge shot into the back bunker. I took one step to the left and my caddie said, "No, we've got to go this way," and he wheeled me to the right. Every golfer wants to walk over the famous Hogan Bridge. But I'd hit it so far right, I had to walk over the Byron Nelson Bridge to get to the green. I never set foot on the Hogan Bridge.

Angered at the triple on 12, which included three putts from 10 feet, I roped a drawing drive up the right side with the beautiful contours of the 13th fairway and I felt better quickly. It was, albeit, merely a temporary moment of euphoria.

"Let's get a birdie on this hole," Mac Williams, my caddie with 23 years at Augusta National at the time, said to me. "Let's birdie this hole."

Easy for him to say.

With that, I promptly shanked a 5-iron right and then hit another 5-iron into Rae's Creek, winding up with a triple-bogey 8.

By the time I left Amen Corner, I was afraid of every club in my bag, as if each one were an enemy plotting to ruin my life.

I was a pitiful mass of humanity by No. 15, where I found yet more water. From the middle of the fairway after a good drive, trying to get the ball to the green on 15 with water in the front and back looks as difficult as trying to land a 767 onto the George Washington Bridge. It felt that tight.

How rattled was I at that point?

I looked at the "Through 14:" scoreboard along the 15th fairway and realized if my name was up there, it would read: "Through 14: Mark Cannizzaro +28."

It was a horrific performance at this golf cathedral, where the fairways and greens are perfect and without a weed in sight, and some of the bunkers with their white sand look like ocean waves rolling toward you.

I went from the euphoric feeling of being in heaven to the angst of hell in 18 holes, yet I'd never been so happy shooting a 113 after following my front-nine 49 with an unthinkable 64 on the back.

I was embarrassed by my performance, disgusted at not being able to produce my "A" game for what should have been the round of my life. But I also was grateful for having had the opportunity to have been there to do it in the first place.

A most fitting twist to my day: after putting out for yet another disappointing double bogey on 18 to finish my round, I dropped a ball to the spot where O'Meara drained his 20-footer to win the Masters the day before and nailed it dead center. It was the longest putt I hit all day.

I walked away desperate for another shot at Augusta National, because I felt I had a score or two to settle.

Two years later, I would get my chance to even the score.

After the 2000 Masters, I actually snuck my way onto Augusta National. I cannot tell you how, because I must protect my sources. Anyway, that's irrelevant. The point is, I was getting the chance to redeem myself with a round that began on the 10th tee.

That fateful April day in '98, stricken with a virus-like case of the shanks, I went around Augusta National with tears in my eyes because I had been reduced to a mass of frightened humanity.

When I left that day, I'd desperately hoped to play Augusta again. Someday. It was inhuman, after all, to subject a passionate golfer to a one-off chance while he's got the shanks. That's like bringing a starving guy with his jaw wired shut to a one-time-only all-you-can-eat lobster buffet.

Without as much as a practice swing, I crushed a drawing drive off the 10th tee that rolled to the bottom of the fairway hill at precisely 8:45 AM the morning after the 2000 Masters that Vijay Singh had just won.

I took a double on 10 despite the good drive and Amen Corner awaited. The iconic three-hole stretch I'd played in 8-over par two years prior. There were demons to be exorcised.

What would transpire for the next 40 minutes or so I can only theorize was by the grace of God. I was heroic through Amen Corner, where Singh nearly threw away the green jacket the day before.

I smashed a drive almost to the drop area on 11, punched a 7-iron to the front of the green and 3-putted from about 70 feet for bogey. Singh was in the water on his second shot the day before. I was on the green.

On 12, a place where I'd shanked a 6-iron so far right two years ago that I never got a chance to walk over the fabled Hogan Bridge, I stiffed a 6-iron over the Rae's Creek, over the bunker and onto the green.

After savoring the walk over the Hogan Bridge and entering the utter serenity of the 12th green, I fixed the ball mark from my shot (never have I taken such pleasure in fixing a ball mark in my life) and 2-putted for par.

On 13, I nuked another huge, drawing drive and had 220 to the pin. From there, I flushed a 5-wood over Rae's Creek and just off the green to the left and ended up parring the hole.

I'd settled the score; 1-over around Amen Corner—a seven-shot improvement from the last time I'd been there. This was one of the thrills of my life.

What I would do the rest of the round mattered little. I'd conquered Augusta's daunting Amen Corner.

I ended up shooting 97 (shaving some 16 shots off the previous effort). I finished the memorable day with only three pars and had 38 putts. But my performance on Amen Corner left me with immeasurable satisfaction. I left the grounds quietly and with a smile painted to my face as if it had been me, not Singh, who'd won the green jacket.

SOURCES

Newspapers and Periodicals
Associated Press
Augusta Chronicle
Huffington Post
Los Angeles Times
New York Post
New York Times
Pittsburgh Post-Gazette
Sports Illustrated
Wall Street Journal

Television
Golf Channel

Websites
Golf Channel.com
NJ.com
PGATour.com

ACKNOWLEDGMENTS

Special thanks to: Phil Mickelson, who was kind enough to write the foreword for this book and for being so generous with his valuable time being interviewed for it.

New York Post (particularly Greg Gallo, my first sports editor, and Chris Shaw, my current sports editor) for assigning me to golf, which has sent me to the past 25 Masters and more than 100 major championships in my 26 years at the newspaper.

Paul Azinger, who provides colorful and insightful analysis on anything and everything golf related…and on plenty of other topics, as well.

Scott Michaux and David "Ghost" Westin, both of whom worked tirelessly at the *Augusta Chronicle* for years delivering the most comprehensive coverage any annual big sporting event has ever gotten.

Charles Howell III, who is one of the most enjoyable and insightful interviews in golf.

Ernie Els, who is one of the most honest interviews in golf.

Mark Cumins, the owner of TBonz Steakhouse, the unofficial Masters 19th hole.

Tiger Woods, who's as responsible for me (and countless golf-writing colleagues) covering as much golf as I have since his dramatic arrival in 1997 and subsequent dominance since.

Oliver Katcher, who should own a patent on the Masters fan experience.

Also helpful through various interviews:

Brian Bush	John Daly
Scott Brown	Zach Johnson
Andy North	David Love III
Jim Nantz	Rickie Fowler
Joe LaCava	Nick Watney
Jim "Bones" Mackay	Brandt Snedeker
Keegan Bradley	Paul Casey
Jim Furyk	Peter Jacobson
Jack Nicklaus	Fuzzy Zoeller
Gary Player	Geoff Ogilvy
Tony Finau	Nathan Grube
Gary Woodland	Jay Danzi
Brendan Steele	Mark O'Meara
Jordan Spieth	Jimmy Roberts
Jason Day	Curtis Strange
Ian Poulter	Nick Faldo
Adam Scott	Patrick Reed

Bernhard Langer

Charl Schwartzel

David Duval

Justin Thomas

Xander Schauffele

Francesco Molinari

Brooks Koepka

Rory McIroy

Gerry McIlroy

Gabby Maguire

Colm McIlroy

Paul Gray

Danny Willett

Justin Rose

Sergio García

Angela Akins

Paul McGinley

Lee Westwood

Duffy Waldorf

Scott McCarron

Joe Damiano

Billy Payne

Greg Norman

Fred Couples

Colin Montgomerie

Steve Stricker

Costantino Rocca

Nick Price

Ben Crenshaw

Jimmy Walker

Webb Simpson

Morgan Hoffmann